SUSTAINABLE DEVELOPMENT OF HILL AREA BY TEA CULTIVATION

A Study in the Nilgiris District

M.B. PRANESH

Foreword by
Prof. M.S. Swaminathan

Publications

KALPAZ PUBLICATIONS
DELHI-110052

Sustainable Development of Hill Area by Tea Cultivation

Rs. 750

ISBN: 81-7835-426-8

Published in 2005 in India by
Kalpaz Publications,
C-30, Satyawati Nagar, Delhi-110052
E-mail : Kalpaz@hotmail.com

Laser Typesetting at : Master Computers, Delhi
Printed at : Salasar Imaging System, Delhi

SUSTAINABLE DEVELOPMENT OF HILL AREA BY TEA CULTIVATION

Dedicated to the memory of my parents
Shri M.S. Bheema Rao
and
Smt. Sumitrabai

Contents

Foreword

The quality of life and human security in the plains of India depend heavily on the ecological security of mountain and hill ecosystems. Apart from the traditional belief that hills are the abode of God, they play a vital role in regulating hydrologic systems and in the origin of major rivers. The Western Ghats, for example, is the source of origin of three major rivers - Krishna, Godavari and Cauveri. Hills are the habitats of wildlife and biodiversity. Hill soils are rich in micro-flora and micro-fauna. Many medicinal plants and herbs as well as herbal healing traditions originate from the hills. Rich cultural and biodiversity co-exist in the hill areas and a majority of tribal families still live in such areas. It has therefore been an act of vision and wisdom on the part of Dr M B Pranesh that he chose the Nilgiris District of Tamil Nadu for a detailed analysis of the present environmental scenario and for preparing a road map for the sustainable development and management of this unique hill ecosystem, which was identified for designating the first Biosphere Reserve in India. Sustainable development requires concurrent attention to the principles of ecology, social and gender equity, ecological economics and employment generation. In the area of equity, we should consider not only the needs of the present generation (i.e., intra-generational), but also of the generations yet to be born (i.e., intergenerational).

The Author has described in detail the human-nature interaction in the Nilgiris district, with a view to developing a strategy for natural resources management which will help to promote not only harmony between man and nature, but also harmony among the different cultural and ethnic groups inhabiting the hills - both tribals and non-tribals.

Anthropogenic pressures are increasing in the Nilgiris district. The Author has therefore examined in detail the impact of the Hill Area Development Programme (HADP) which is being implemented in the district since 1975. HADP aims to achieve eco-restoration, eco-preservation and ecodevelopment This will call for detailed attention to ecologically sound land use practices. Since soil erosion and land slides are serious problems, HADP has promoted a shift in land use from annual crops like vegetables and potato to perennial crops like tea. As a result, the area under Tea increased from 38,454 ha in 1986-87 to 48.954 ha in 1996-97. Dr Pranesh presents in this book data on the pattern of this switch from annual crops to tea. He has provided valuable information on the economics of tea cultivation and the impact of the altered land use patterns brought about by HADP on employment and income.

The book also contains Dr Pranesh's observations on the impact of HADP in the Darjeeling district of West Bengal. Darjeeling tea is world famous and there also, Dr Pranesh has observed the beneficial impact of HADP. Darjeeling, unlike the Nilgiris is characterized by the preponderance of large tea gardens. The forest areas both in the Nilgiris and Darjeeling are tending to shrink. The current coverage of forests in these districts are 44.5% in Darjeeling and 56.3% in the Nilgiris district. The ecological aim of HADP should be to conserve the forest area without any further diversion to other uses and restore degraded forests.

This book is a timely contribution to the ecological and economic management of hill areas. I hope it will be widely used by scholars and policy makers for formulating sustainable development strategies for the hill and mountain regions of our country. We are indebted to Dr M B Pranesh for this labour of love for ecological and humn centred economics.

M S Swaminathan

Preface

Sustainable Development has been defined as 'Development that meets the needs of the present generation without compromising the ability of future generations to meet their needs'. Hill Areas are fragile eco-systems. The ecology of the hills has to be preserved for the benefit of people living in the hills as well as the plains, whose rainfall and climate are dependant on the hills. The hills contain valuable minerals, flora and fauna to be used by present as well as future generations. Local population in the hills is generally poor and is in need of economic development. While economic development activities should be allowed, they should not result in deterioration of the ecology of the hills. Hence the concept of sustainable development is very relevant for Hill areas.

My work as Planning Secretary to the Government of Tamil Nadu for three years, gave me the opportunity to supervise the Hill Area Development Programme and the Western Ghats Development Programme. I benefited from many interactions with the Union Planning Commission, which formulates and guides implementation of these schemes. I had opportunity to tour extensively through the Hill Areas covered by these programmes. Participation in a conference on Sustainable Village Based Development in the Colorado State University, USA helped me widen my vision and deepen my understanding of Sustainable Development.

The HADP is being implemented in the Nilgiris district to promote economic development of the people in the hills, while also protecting the ecosystem through conservation, reclamation and restoration. HADP adopts the Watershed approach. Based on Remote sensing techniques, Watersheds in the Nilgiris district have been delineated and 75 Watersheds chosen for development on priority. Most of the funds are invested on programmes to benefit the priority Watersheds.

While the HADP supports many sectors, its main emphasis has been on Afforestation, Soil Conservation and Horticulture. Afforestation programme seeks to restore the forest cover. The Soil Conservation programme seeks to preserve top-soil which is steadily getting eroded. The Horticulture programme encourages cultivation of ecologically appropriate crops like tea and fruit trees.

Nilgiris district has a substantial area under cultivation of potato, other vegetables and seasonal crops. These require tilling of the soil before each planting season. The rains that follow, carry away a substantial amount of top-soil. Cultivation of tea does not require ploughing of the land after the tea bushes are established. Hence there is no loss of top-soil every year. Thus substitution of seasonal crops by tea, results in reduction of soil erosion. Farmers receive good and steady income from sale of tea-leaves throughout the year. The economic condition of farmers improves while degradation of soil is arrested. Thus cultivation of tea instead of seasonal crops, promotes sustainable development of the people and protects their land. For this reason, HADP has promoted substitution of seasonal crops by tea.

Farmers are assisted by HADP in shaping the land for tea cultivation. They are given tea-clones at subsidized rates. A co-operative federation of tea-factories has been strengthened to help small farmers in marketing their tea-leaves. Expenditure under HADP towards the above schemes has promoted tea cultivation in the district. During the eighties and nineties, the area under tea cultivation in the Nilgiris district increased rapidly. In addition to HADP, some other factors also encouraged tea cultivation. One of them was the attractive price fetched by tea-leaves. Tea Board also implemented a scheme to help small farmers. Problems associated with potato cultivation could also have encouraged tea cultivation. Thus many factors could have contributed to the increase in tea-area. My research study aimed at estimating the role of HADP in achieving the desired change in cropping pattern.

Two methods were used for estimating the contribution of HADP. One was the analytical method. Secondary data was used to build a regression model for the tea area in a year as a function of the expenditure under HADP, the price fetched by tea-leaves and other factors. From the co-efficients in the regression equation, the role of HADP was estimated.

The second method was by collection of primary data from a field study. A stratified random sample of about 500 farmers was designed to represent the small tea growers of Nilgiris district. The sample farmers were interviewed using a pre-tested questionnaire. The farmers were asked to rank HADP and other factors which motivated them to substitute tea for the crop grown earlier. Analysing their responses, a second estimate for the role of HADP was obtained.

Taking note of the results obtained by the two methods, the contribution of HADP was estimated. The study showed that HADP had played a significant and very important role in the expansion of Tea area in the district.

The field study yielded a lot of data about the composition of the small farmers, their holdings, when they started cultivating tea, the crop which they cultivated earlier, etc. During study of secondary data, I could collect a good deal of information relating to development of the concepts of Sustainable development, objectives of the Union Planning Commission in promoting Hill Area Development, formulation of State Level Plan and problems in implementation at the district level. Much data about the Nilgiris district and the growth of tea cultivation in the district were also put together.

My study materials also included historical information about the district. A gazetteer written a hundred years ago and a research work of 1875, gave pictures of the district as it then was and perception of scholars at that time. It was curious to observe that many of the concerns being voiced now, were being voiced then also. There was also an account of the rise and fall of coffee cultivation in the district during the 1860's. That would make one wonder whether tea cultivation would also have to suffer a fall one day, like coffee did.

For horizontal comparison, I made a visit to Darjeeling district. This district, famous for its tea, has many points of similarity with the Nilgiris. There are also differences. Both districts are covered under HADP. But the priorities in the Darjeeling Plan are quite different from those in the Nilgiris.

After 1999, the tea-leaf prices fell steeply. After many years of boom, the farmers had to go through gloomy years during which prices were low and returns poor. This created unrest in the district. The Government of Tamil Nadu, Government of India and the Tea Board took a number of steps to help the tea cultivators. However the scene still remain gloomy. Farmers are waiting for the return of the good old days of good tea prices. In the meanwhile, the area under Tea continues to grow.

I have acknowledged elsewhere the sources of secondary data and the help received from a large number of persons in completing this study. Limitations of the study have also been mentioned elsewhere. Some errors may remain in this work. Responsibility for them is entirely mine. I crave the indulgence of discerning readers.

After my thesis was accepted by Pondicherry University, my guide Prof. K. Ramachandran suggested that it could be brought out as a book, since there were not many books on this subject. His encouragement has emboldened me to present this book. I hope it will be found useful by students of Sustainable Hill Area Development.

M.B. PRANESH

Acknowledgements

Prof. M.S. Swaminathan is well known all over the world as an authority on the subject of Sustainable Development. It is my good fortune that he has been kind enough to write the Foreword for this book. I am deeply grateful to him.

This book is a slightly modified version of my thesis accepted by the Pondicherry University for award of the degree of Ph.D. (Economics).

I am deeply grateful to Dr. K. Ramachandran, Retired Senior Professor of Economics and Director, Pondicherry University Community College, Pondicherry, who kindly acted as my guide in planning the research, collecting the reference material, planning the econometric and empirical studies and analyzing the results for my Ph.D. thesis. I also thank Prof. Sham Bhat, Head of the Department of Economics, Pondicherry University for his help and suggestions.

I am very grateful to Dr. N. Malathi, Professor of Economics, Annamalai University, Dr. S. Perumalsamy, Professor and Head, Department of Economics, Bharathiar University, Coimbatore and Dr. K. Badrinarayanan, Lecturer in School of Business, Singapore who kindly appraised the thesis and gave their reports.

I thank the Government of Tamil Nadu for having kindly accorded permission to me to register for the Ph.D.

programme and granted access to material regarding Hill Area Development Programme in the Nilgiris. The Planning and Development Department, Department of Evaluation and Applied Research and the Department of Economics and Statistics of the Government of Tamil Nadu, Collectorate and the HADP Cell of the Nilgiris District in Ootacamund, INCOSERVE, Tea Board, TANTEA and UPASI in Coonoor have provided valuable information. So have officers of many Departments in the Nilgiris District.

I wish to record with gratitude the help received from the following persons in obtaining the data, processing the information and completing data entry, word processing and preparation of the report:

M/s. M.A. Gowrishankar, IAS., and R. Santhanam, IAS., Secretaries to Government, Planning and Development Department, K. Sonai, IAS., Collector of Nilgiris, Dhiraj Kumar, IAS., Pradeep Yadav, IAS., Project Directors and Balusamy of HADP Cell, Ooty, Vishwanath Shegaonkar, IAS., Dayanand Kataria, IAS., Managing Directors, Pitchaimuthu and Manivannan of INCOSERVE, Coonoor, N. Ramadurai, Secretary General, UPASI, Somasekhar, IFS., and A. Roy Choudhury of the Tea Board Regional Office, Coonoor, Dr. Sikka of the Central Soil and Water Conservation Research and Training Institute, Ooty, Dr. K. Rajaram, Deputy Director, Geo-Technical Cell, Coonoor, M. Raman, Shanmugham and Syed Khader Ali of the Department of Horticulture, Ooty, Halan A. of TANTEA, Coonoor, Palaniswamy of Agriculture Engineering Department, Ooty, Ayyappan of the Coffee Board Gudalur Dr. Baskaran, IAS., Director and Smt. Ananthalakshmi, Joint Director, Department of Economics and Statistics, Chennai, Dr. R. Natarajan and Dr. Udayabhaskar of Madras University, Balasubramanian and Lakshminarayanan of MEPZ, J. Suresh, M. Chandrasekaran and B. Ravichandran of TACID, Tmt. T.V. Kousalya and Thiru T. Shanmugasundaram of the Tamil Nadu Government Secretariat.

Lakshmi Pranesh, Madhukar, Jayanth, Kavita, Venkatesh, Aarathi and the MB family have been of immense support to me in sustaining my effort during the long time it took to complete the thesis and bring out this book.

I thank all the above and many others, who helped me in one way or another.

M.B. PRANESH

1

Introduction

The most challenging problem which our country has to face in the coming decades will be to provide food, health and economic security to the millions of our population. This requires a careful matching of technological vectors with social dynamics to improve the carrying capacity of the country through the optimal management of its natural resources. The challenge is to build up sustainable regenerative capacity of the land and water resources to provide basic food and economic security to the people at large, without compromising on the ecological and environmental integrity.

Explosive growth of human population, particularly in the developing countries like India, has led to severe encroachment of forest and grass lands. The deforestation of over 10 million hectares of closed forest in India during 1973-1983 reduced the closed forest cover from 14 per cent to a meagre 11 per cent of our geographical area in 1997-98. Awareness of the extent of severe deforestation dramatically brought about by space remote sensing has helped in arresting further depletion. But a lot of damage has already been done. Inevitable consequences of large scale deforestation have been depletion of top soil, severe degradation of land, sedimentation of water bodies and increased run-off of rain water, resulting in increasing desertification of marginal lands and flooding of rivers. The annual sedimentation load carried by just the Ganges and the Brahmaputra alone exceeds 2000 MT, almost a quarter of the total sedimentation load transported by all the rivers in the world.

The key to the achievement of sustainable integrated development is the adoption of environment friendly, scientific and technological approach for achieving rapid progress. Advances in agricultural sciences and biotechnology and phenomenal progress in space technology have made it possible to improve the global as well as local carrying capacity to meet the present and projected needs of future generations without impairing ecological and environmental integrity. Mankind now has the technology and the opportunity to replace the old practice and mindless exploitation of the planet earth with a new culture of sustainable, integrated development to enable humankind as a whole to have a common future.[1]

Development

The term "Development" covers everything from economic to social, cultural and political change. It pertains to goals, tasks and processes. The underlying assumption and values of mainstream development thinking are based on values of classical liberalism. The idea of progress is central for the modernization theory. According to this theory, the world is composed of two types of society – traditional and modern – with the former emulating the latter. Traditional, essentially rural societies are underdeveloped and have not yet made the transition from subsistence to commercial agriculture. These societies are also technologically backward, which limits their control over the environment.

Mainstream modernization theory of development suffers from inherent ecological incompatibility. It does not have a wise relationship to the earth and her resources. It systematically produces marginal people who have no meaningful roles in the society.

Participatory Development

Participatory development has also been called authentic development. It is a process by which the people of a society develop themselves and the institutions in their society that enhance their ability to mobilize and manage available resources to produce sustainable and justly distributed improvements in the quality of life consistent with their own aspirations. In this concept of development, the focus is not on economic growth, but on people and their advancement as a whole. A participatory strategy for promoting development proceeds on the assumption that people have more to contribute to the development process than just their money or labour. They have ideas, management skills, technical insights and organizational capabilities needed for development. They are to be regarded as partners more than 'beneficiaries' or 'target groups'. They should have an active role in selecting and implementing schemes for benefiting the locality.

Eco-development

No issue is more central or vital to the lives of people in the Third world than protection of the environment. Unlike industrial societies, which possess technology and complex social systems, traditional societies cannot survive apart from the natural environment. They live within a bio-mass based subsistence economy. Fundamental needs like food, fuels, building materials, fertilizers and raw materials are all forms of bio-mass, most of which are collected free from the immediate environment. True development is synonymous with sustainability. Eco-development should aim at protection of the remaining Eco-system through conservation, reclamation and restoration.[2]

Decades of vigorous pursuit of economic development, has exposed the dark side of the development process.

Intensification of agriculture has in fact, brought about soil erosion, desertification, water-logging, contamination of surface and ground water by fertilizers and pesticides, etc. Industrial production in turn has led to large-scale emission of carbon-di-oxide, methane, chlorofluoro carbons and other gases, which have contributed to the 'green-house effect'. The above problems have created awareness about the need for sustainable development.

Sustainable Development

Sustainable development would call for increases in productivity and efficiency of the existing land, water, flora and fauna resources in a planned manner without jeopardizing their future use. In general, renewable resources like water, forests and fisheries, can be used to the extent of their ability to renew themselves through natural growth. Sustainable development implies that the environmental capital stocks should be held constant over time. There are certain ecological limits beyond which exploitation of these natural resources would not be sustainable. The main objectives of sustainable development can be stated to be environmental harmony, economic efficiency, equity with social justice both intra and inter-generational, conservation of resources and local self-reliance.[3]

With the catastrophe at Chernobyl in 1986, the world glimpsed the abyss, the destructive potential for global environment pollution and degradation of modern industrial development. Six years later, at Rio de Janeiro in 1992, the Earth Summit presented a programme for action to avert global environmental disaster based on the underlying principles of sustainable development. This process of global negotiation and agreement on environmental problems culminated in the adoption of 27 principles constituting a Declaration on Environment and Development, the first of which was 'Human beings are at the center of concerns for sustainable development'. By consensus, the summit endorsed Agenda 21, an 800 pages action programme for following up the agreements reached at the Earth Summit.

Sustainable development has now passed a threshold of public and political concern that makes it fully and permanently established as an issue of high priority on the national and international policy making agenda.[4]

The term "sustainability" and its corollary "sustainable development" are being widely used in Government policy pronouncements, scientific articles, publications of international aid agencies, professional literature, seminar, symposia and popular media. However, they convey different meanings to different people. The view point of the developing countries differs considerably from that of the developed countries as evidenced in the Rio summit. The developing countries are mainly concerned with tackling the immediate economic problems and eliminating poverty, whereas the developed countries' thrust is on combating industry related pollution and maintaining the attained economic level.

The report of the World Commission on Environment and Development, [5] Our Common Future (also known as the Bruntland Commission Report) generated worldwide discussion on the theme of sustainable development. In broad terms, the essential concerns of sustainable development are:

1. Survival of human beings.
2. Survival of all other life forms.
3. Satisfaction of basic human needs.
4. Maintenance of bio-physical productivity.
5. Economic efficiency and growth.
6. Preservation of environmental quality and ecosystem.
7. Inter and intra-generational equity.
8. Social justice.

9. Self-reliance and people's participation.
10. Stabilization of human population.
11. Promotion of values and ethics.

As a result of the wide-ranging debate on sustainable Development, consensus is emerging on the following points.

1. Excessive stress on bio-physical environment for short term gain is ultimately counter productive, i.e., there is a limit to which productivity can be raised.
2. Human survival can only be ensured by preserving the basic resource base.
3. Even the renewable resources are not perpetual unless prudent management praxis is followed.
4. Social justice and equity are prime objectives of any form of development so far conceived. Quite naturally they are also the professed goals of Sustainable Development.[6]

Ecosystems are the sources of water, of animal and plant food and of other renewable resources. They maintain a genetic library, sustain the processes that preserve and regenerate soil, recycle nutrients, control floods, filter pollutants, assimilate waste, pollinate crops, operate the hydrological cycle and maintain the gaseous composition of the atmosphere. The totality of all ecosystems represents our natural capital base or the Environmental Resource Base (ERB).

Biological diversity provides the system its functional properties and its resilience. Degradation of ERB by excessive resource-extraction or severe land use affects the quantity and quality of services produced by the ecosystem. It also challenges the resilience of the ecosystem to recover from perturbations, shocks and surprises. If a system loses its resilience, it can flip to a wholly new state. The 'carrying capacity' is the maximum stress which the ecosystem is capable of absorbing without flipping to a vastly different state.

Carrying capacity of the ecosystem does not remain constant, but is subject to change in unpredictable ways. Economic policies that apply fixed rules to achieve constant yields, can be expected to lead to a reduction in the resilience of the ecosystem.

Environmental problems are associated with renewable resources that are in danger of exhaustion from excessive use – atmosphere, animal, bird, plant and fish populations. Land is also such a commodity. Availability of arable and grazing land can be maintained only by careful use. Overuse by unsustainably short fallow periods, deforestation, cultivation and grazing of marginal lands, causes the quality of land to deteriorate. Eventually it becomes a wasteland. Under natural conditions of vegetation cover, it can take 100 to 500 years for the formation of 1 cm of top-soil. Due to wind and water run-off, the topsoil can be lost into water bodies and non-agricultural land. This erosion is to be distinguished from loss of soil nutrients and humus which can be made up by applying fertilizers (which however can have adverse effects elsewhere in the ecosystem). Soil degradation can occur if the wrong crops are cultivated. Export crops such as coffee and tea enjoy a continuous root-structure and provide continuous canopy cover. With grasses planted underneath, the rate of erosion is less than that associated with basic food crops.

Environmental resources such as forests are multifunctional and have competing uses. Forests provide timber, fibre, paper, oils, soaps, pharmaceuticals and habitat for a rich genetic pool. They influence local and regional climate, preserve soil cover on site and in the case of watersheds, protect soil downstream from floods. Deforestation leads to increased run-off, stripping of soil, depriving agricultural nutrients and clogging irrigation systems.[7]

Sustainable development has been criticized as a catch-all offering different meanings to different interests. It has been adopted enthusiastically by environmentalists and is now commonplace in official reports and a slogan for politicians. Business has enthusiastically embraced it to help legitimize its activities. It would be a mistake to dismiss sustainable development as mere platitude or just the fashion of the day soon to disappear like the concern about "limits to growth" of an earlier era. For one thing many of the issues, the depletion of resources, the growth of population, the increase of pollution, the degradation of soil, habitats and species are recurrent themes. They threaten the planet's overall carrying capacity and the ability of its ecosystems to regenerate themselves. By linking development and environment, the needs and aspirations of the developing world have been incorporated. It has become apparent that environmental issues cannot be dealt with in isolation. They are interdependent parts of a greater whole. Strenuous efforts are being made to define, interpret and introduce sustainable development at local, national and global levels. The most generally accepted definition of sustainable development is the following terse one given by the Bruntland Commission–

> "Sustainable development is development that meets the needs of the present without compromising the ability of future generations to meet their own needs."

Sustainable development is essentially a planning process with definite goals and priorities. The scale of operation is as important as the methodology itself. In the case of sustainable development, it is considered both pragmatic and rational to shift to Local Level Planning – the Panchayat, the lowest administrative unit in India. Some reasons indicating this are:

1. It is a fact that environmental degradation and socio-economic problems are expressed mostly at the local level. As the problems are manifested at the local level, they have to be tackled there itself. Involvement of local communities of actual users is necessary to achieve best results.
2. A local user inheriting traditional wisdom is most aware about the problems and potentialities of his land.
3. Actual users must be made aware about the draw back of the current practices and the positive relationship between environment and development.

Hill area Development

Traditional agriculture in mountain areas has relied primarily on locally available natural resources and their management, for meeting food, fodder, fibre and fuel needs. Crops, livestock and forestry have formed an integral part of the farming system in mountain areas. In adapting to the specific needs of greatly varying slopes, aspects, climates and soils over short distances, farming systems in mountain areas have to consider important points like maintenance of soil fertility, control of soil erosion, management of water-resources and management of forest resources.[8]

With the last 10 years, there has been a rapid growth of population in hill areas. This growth has put more pressure on the farming system to meet food, fodder and fuel needs. Hill areas supported a moderate population in earlier times. But with successful control of malaria, the population in hill areas is growing fast. This has resulted in uneconomic fragmentation of holdings.

Unmanaged growth of livestock has resulted in excessive deforestation and over-grazing. Increasing number of livestock is a major threat to sustainability of hill areas.

Penetration of market forces into the hills has brought many advantages but also, some disadvantages. Market demand for timber and forest produce, has accelerated extraction of trees. Changes in land policies have had a significant influence on land based resources. A review of land policies indicates that land and forest policies were used to generate more revenue for the Government. It is only in recent years that the policy shows concerns for sustainable management of available natural resources.

The degree of access has been an important factor in the process of change. With improved access, even remote areas with low population density are experiencing increasing population and market penetration. Both these take a heavy toll on natural resources. Improved access has also led to introduction of market based inputs and commercialization of agriculture. It has facilitated introduction of improved technologies for crops, horticulture, livestock and agro-forestry. Production is less for the farmer's own consumption and more for distant markets. As dependence on external input and knowledge increases, farmers find it more profitable to buy food grains and focus on the most suitable high value crop.

Diversity makes it imperative that hill area development programmes have a wide base of technology in order to have beneficial inputs on different groups. Investment in infrastructure is vital. But it must be selective to make the best use of limited funds and other resources. Infrastructure such as roads, can do little to help farmers where soils are poor. In contrast, roads provide good return to areas with good land and agro climatic conditions.

Mountain people appear to be rapidly accepting mono-cropping, urbanization and commercialization. They demand modern knowledge and improved technology. Overcoming poverty appears to be a higher priority for mountain farmers than concern for the environment, while Government programmes tend to give a higher priority to environmental issues.

Double Green Revolution

The International Policy Research Institute, Washington looked ahead 25 years and projected in 1995, a vision for the food environment in the year 2020. It has come up with a projection of annual deficit of 61 million tons of food by 2020. The institute has called for policy initiatives in time to close the expected deficit. At the global meeting by their institute, a new nomenclature called 'Double Green Revolution' was introduced by Gordon Conway. He referred to a new Green Revolution – one that will be a productive as the past revolution, but will be environmentally friendly and hence sustainable.[9]

The concept of double green revolution is very relevant for mountain agriculture. This is because the growing number of people in the hills, is predominantly poor, malnourished, lacking in food security and living in very fragile environments highly susceptible to frequent natural disasters. Another important point is that increasing pressures on fragile areas, such as mountain, only result in degrading those environments and transferring pressures to other areas. Deterioration in upstream conditions has resulted in catastrophes downstream. Managing mountains and mountain agriculture is therefore, a critical component of the food security system of the lower lands, which depend on water resources originating in mountains.

Hill area development in India

Hill Areas of India whose ecology is fragile, have a crucial role in determining the ultimate rainfall and availability of water for the whole country. Preservation of the hills is necessary not only for the benefit of the people living in the hills but also for the benefit of people living in the plains. At the same time, the interests of the people living in the hills cannot be neglected. They need programmes which can help the people to improve their economic condition. Hence, the concept of sustainable development, is highly relevant to the hill areas of India.

Beneficial Effects of Crop Diversification

In the hill areas, agriculture is the key sector for employment and income-generation because large-scale industrialization is not ecologically desirable and the infrastructure is too poor to attract industries. Traditional crops have little growth potential. Hence emphasis has been laid on promotion of horticultural crops. There is a view that requirement of packing material for marketing horticultural produce will lead to damage to forests. However, detailed studies have found that these negative effects are not considerable. Demand for packing cases is no longer met by cutting timber from local forests. Diversification through horticultural crops has resulted in positive effects like reduction in crop intensity, soil erodibility, livestock pressure and grazing incidence and improvement in income, all of which have favourable ecological implications. Forests in the vicinity of economically improved village suffer less damage than forests near economically more backward villages. Low income and poverty are the major causes for degradation of natural resources. Improvement in socio-economic conditions brought about by diversion to horticultural crops benefits people as well as ecology.[10]

Cultivation of Tea

In particular, diversification of cultivation from annual crops to cultivation of tea, aids sustainable development of hill areas. Annual tilling causes loss of valuable top-soil, where annual crops are cultivated. This causes irreparable damage to the farmers, by loss of fertility of the soil. It also reduces the storage capacity of hydro-electric and irrigation reservoirs located in the foot-hills. If the crop is substituted by tea, water loss can be greatly reduced. There is also a tremendous improvement in the economic condition of small growers due to diversification from annual crops to tea. This has resulted in improvement in living standards. The promotion of tea-cultivation has not only helped in the eco-preservation of the hills, but also brought about economic improvement among the farming community.[11]

The Union Planning Commission has been monitoring and funding a special programme for development of selected hill districts. The programme is called the 'Hill Area Development Programme' (HADP). Guidelines for implementation of the programme have been evolved and elaborated by the Planning Commission in successive Five Year Plans.

Study Area

In the State of Tamil Nadu, the Hill Area Development Programme is being implemented in the Nilgiris District. This district is endowed with such a large diversity of flora and fauna that it has been chosen by UNESCO under its "Man and Biosphere" programme. Its excellent climate and enchanting scenery created by lofty peaks, natural forests and grasslands attract a large number of tourists. The Hill Area Development Programme has been implemented in this district for over two decades. The HADP in the Nilgiris pursues the goals of eco-restoration, eco-preservation and eco-development through development schemes covering many sectors of development. However, the three most important sectors are Forestry, Soil Conservation and Horticulture. Outlay on these sectors has accounted for about 54 per cent of the total outlay in recent years. Horticulture alone has accounted for over 14 per cent of the outlay.

Cultivation of vegetables and seasonal crops is practised over a considerable area of Nilgiris district. Cultivation of seasonal crops involves ploughing of the land every year. Such ploughing leads to disturbance of the top soil. Subsequent rain tends to carry away large amounts of top soil. Nilgiris district is witnessing a great deal of soil erosion. Many programmes have been taken up to arrest soil erosion. Among them, the most important is one of substituting annual crops by tea, which is a perennial crop. Once the tea-bushes are established, there is no need to plough the soil. The root system of the bushes also holds the soil together and minimizes soil erosion. Hence, there is significant reduction in erosion when cultivation of a seasonal crop is substituted by cultivation of tea. For this reason, HADP has laid great emphasis on tea cultivation.

Farmers wanting to shift to tea cultivation are assisted in many ways by HADP. For development of the land to suit tea cultivation, a small farmer can avail himself of schemes under Soil Conservation Sector. The HADP is funding maintenance of nurseries for raising tea clones, which are subsequently distributed to small farmers at subsidized rates. Fertilizers and plant protection chemicals are also given at subsidized prices. HADP is also assisting Industrial Cooperatives of small farmers in processing and marketing tea. Thus HADP has invested in tea related schemes in a number of sectors to promote shift from cultivation of seasonal crops to cultivation of tea.

HADP is in operation in the Nilgiris district since 1975. Starting from the 1980's, there has been a steep increase in the area under tea cultivation in the district. During the reference period 1986-87 to 1996-97, area under tea increased from 38,454 to 48,954 Ha. During this period, annual expenditure by HADP on tea related schemes increased from Rs. 187.77 lakhs to Rs. 576.26 lakhs.

Credit has to be given to HADP for the increase in tea area mentioned above. However, there have been some other favourable factors also, which assisted to increase the area under tea. One of the important factors is the boom in tealeaf prices, which was witnessed during some years within the reference period. The price of tea-leaves, which was Rs. 3.20 per kg in 1986-87 increased in a fluctuating manner to Rs. 6.60 in 1996-97. In between it had touched Rs. 7.66 in 1995-96 and crossed Rs. 6.60 during the years 1989-90, 1990-91 and 1993-94. This has to be recognized as a very important factor motivating farmers to switch over to tea.

There are also other factors like continuous revenue provided by tea for about 10 months of the year, as against one or two harvests of seasonal crops. Tea is also less prone to disease than potato and vegetable crops. Un-remunerative price fetched by potato, coffee and vegetable could have motivated some farmers to switch to tea. Menace due to animals attracted by potato could have motivated some to change over to tea. There could be many other factors like promotional activity by Tea Board and UPASI.

Objectives of the Study

The main purpose of the Study is to estimate the role of HADP in bringing about the increase in area under tea cultivation during the period 1986-87 to 1996-97.

More specifically, the objectives of the study are as follows:

1. Identify the size profile of small farmers who have switched from other crops to tea.
2. Examine the crops which were substituted by tea.
3. Estimate the role of good tea prices in motivating the shift to tea.
4. Test awareness regarding ecological benefit of tea cultivation among tea-farmers.
5. Ascertain the segment of small tea farmers who have availed assistance from HADP tea schemes.
6. Compare the role of HADP assistance and tea price as factors motivating the shift to tea cultivation.
7. Quantify the role of HADP in bringing about substitution of seasonal crops by tea.

Hypothesis

The hypotheses formulated and tested in this study are:

1. There is a positive linear correlation between HADP expenditure on tea related schemes in a year and the extent under tea cultivation in the next year.

2. There is a positive linear correlation between the tea-leaf price in a year and the extent under tea cultivation in the next year.

Sources of Data

The required data for this study have been collected from both primary as well as secondary sources. Primary data have been collected through a well designed pre-tested questionnaire. The questionnaire is designed to elicit the information relating to the size of holding of the farmer, the extent of tea cultivated, when he shifted to tea-cultivation, the crop cultivated earlier, whether he received HADP assistance and his awareness of HADP objectives and also some questions relating to motivation.

Secondary data has been collected from published and unpublished sources like the Department of Horticulture, Department of Statistics and HADP Cell. Data relating to area under tea cultivation was collected from the Tea Board and the Department of Statistics. Data relating to annual expenditure by HADP on various sectors, was collected from the HADP Cell. Annual average figures of tea-leaf prices were collected from INCOSERVE, the Federation of Industrial Cooperative Societies of Small Tea Growers.

Sampling Procedure

The study has been taken up among small Tea farmers of the Nilgiris district. The district has about 30,000 small tea growers holding about 16,000 Ha (40,000 acres) of tea-garden. Of them, over 18,600 farmers holding over 31,000 acres are members of 17 Industrial Cooperative tea factories, located in all the six taluks of the district. Out of these 17, a selection of 11 factories was made, such that all the six taluks of the district were represented. Two factories were selected from each taluk except Gudalur, which has only one INDCO tea factory. Considering the total number of small farmers mentioned above a sample size of 531 was selected. In each factory, convenient samples of about 50 tea farmers was taken. This stratified convenient sample has representation from all taluks. The sample can be used to represent the small farmers of the Nilgiris district. However it would not be safe to draw taluk-wise inferences as the number of respondents in each taluk is small.

Data Analysis

Besides percentage and tabular analysis the collected data has been analysed through correlation and linear regression.

A linear regression Model has been postulated as follows to estimate the tea area as a linear function of four independent variables namely HADP expenditure on tea related schemes, Tea price this year, Potato-price this year and Tea area this year.

$$T_{a+1} = mX_a + nY_a + pZ_a + qT_a + k$$

where X_a = Tea Price this year

Y_a = HADP Expenditure on tea Related Schemes this year

Z_a = Potato Price this year

T_a = Tea area this year

T_{a+1} = Tea area next year

m, n, p, q and k are constants.

Period of Study

The field survey was conducted during March-April 1999

The period taken for the analysis of data from the secondary sources is 1986-87 to 1996-97.

Limitations of the Study

The following limitations need to be kept in view, while considering the findings of this study. The study is based on a sample of 531. The size of the sample is small compared to the total number of about 30,000 small tea farmers. One taluk, Pandalur is not represented among the beneficiaries.

The sample is only a stratified convenient sample. The beneficiaries have not been chosen by a truly random process. They have been chosen conveniently among those who visited INDCO factories during the chosen period.

The study is based on figures for the period 1986-87 to 1996-97. Figures for earlier years have not been used because of apparent errors in data. Entire expenditure on three sectors – soil conservation, horticulture and INDCO Tea factories – has been taken as expenditure having impact on development of tea area. Some of the expenditure may not have benefited tea area development directly.

Price paid for tea leaves varies within the year depending upon the season. The hypothesis has assumed an average price for the year. This assumption may limit the accuracy of the forecast.

A large number of factors influencing the tea area have been lumped into the constant. Consequently about 33 per cent of the dependent variable is not determined by the selected four independent variables. Hence the model serves only a limited purpose of estimating, the role of selected variables. It does not deal with all the factors affecting the tea area.

Chapter frame

Chapter 1 explains the theoretical aspect of the concept of development, sustainable development and Hill Area development followed by the major objective, hypothesis and methodology of study. Chapter 2 reviews the literature on HADP. Chapter 3 gives a brief profile of the study area viz., Nilgiris district. Chapter 4 appraises a macro analysis of the HADP. Chapter 5 describes a micro analysis of HADP in Nilgiris district. Chapter 6 analyses the growth and development of tea cultivation in the Nilgiris. Chapter 7 has an analytical study of the role of HADP in promoting tea cultivation based on secondary data. Chapter 8 analyses the role of HADP in the shift to tea cultivation based on primary data collected by Filed Study. Chapter 9 summarizes the main findings and conclusions. Situation in the Nilgiris has changed dramatically after the year 2000. The present position is briefly indicated in Chapter 10. Historical contrast with the position a century ago is given in Chapter 11. Comparison with another similar hill district is presented in Chapter 12.

References

1. Rao, U.R.(1995), *Statistical Dynamics of Sustainable Development*, Vol. XVII No. 2, June, Centre for Research in Rural and Industrial Development. pp. 1-7.

2. Gohlert Ernest (1993), *Foundation of Sustainable Development*, Proceedings of the International Conference on Sustainable Village Based Development, Colorado State University, Fort Collins USA. pp. 105-138.

3. Pranesh, M.B. (1993), *Sustainable Village Based Development-Central Government Policy-The Indian Picture*, Proceedings of the International Conference on Sustainable Village Based Development, Colorado State University, Fort Collins, USA. pp. 523-538.

4. Blowers Andrew (1995) Environment and Development (Views from the East and the West), Ed. Mukherjee A and Agnihotri, Concept Publishing Co., New Delhi-59. pp. 349-359.

5. WCED(1987), 'Our Common Future', *Report of the World Commission on Environment and Development*, Oxford University Press, New York.

6. Chattopadhyay Srikumar (1995) Environment and Development (views from the East and the West), Ed. Mukherjee A and Agnihotri VK, Concept publishing Co., New Delhi 59. pp. 39-47.

7. Dasgupta Partha et. al (1994) Population, Economic Development and the Environment, Ed. Kieshing KL and Landberg H, Oxford University Press. pp. 164-180.

8. Banskota.M and Partap.T(1996), Education, Research and Sustainable Mountain Agriculture, Priorities for the Hindu Kush Himalayas'. International Centre for Integrated Mountain Development, Kathmandu. pp. 1-32.

9. IFPRI (1995) *A 2020 Vision for Food Environment*, Washington D.C., International Food Policy Research Institute and the National Geographic Society Washing D.C.

10. Chand Ramesh (1998), 'Ecological and Economic impact of horticultural development in the Himalayas', Economic and Political Weekly, June 29, 1998. pp. A93-95.

11. Ramu. S and Ramamurthy. G (1999) "Promotion of Tea Cultivation for crop Diversification in Nilgiris", Paper presented at Workshop organized by HADP Cell, Ootacamund.

2

Review of Literature

The Report 'Our Common Future[1], of the World Commission on Environment and Development traces the evolution and development of the concept of 'Sustainable Development'. It provides the most generally accepted definition of Sustainable Development as development that meets the needs of the present generation without compromising the ability of future generations to meet their own needs.

Srikumar Chattopadhyay[2] has concisely explained the concept of sustainable development. Andrew Blowers (1995)[3] deals with the environment needed for the success of sustainable development. Partha Dasgupta, et. al (1994)[4] elucidate the concepts of Environmental Resource Base and carrying capacity. U.R. Rao (1995)[5] explains the application of space technology in achieving sustainable development.

Ernest Gohlert[6] discusses how mainstream modernization theory of development is incompatible with preservation of the ecology. Stressing that no issue is more vital to developing countries than preservation of the environment, Gohlert argues in favour of participating development.

Pranesh M.B[7], discusses the main objectives of sustainable development.

Banskota and Pratab (1996)[8] discuss the special character of agriculture in hill areas. They also discuss the concept of 'Double Green Revolution' put forth by Gordon Conway in the international conference held in 1995, at Washington DC under the auspices of the Food Policy Research Institute[9], Washington to discuss the 2020 vision for Food and Environment.

Ignacy Sachs' (1995)[10] writing on the challenges of the Social Summit, discusses the need for new development strategies which combine economic, environmental and social objectives.

Benefits of shifting from agriculture to horticulture in hill areas are discussed by Ramesh Chand (1996)[11].

Sustainable Development of Hill Areas has been considered specifically by the Union Planning Commission in the Sixth[12] Seventh[13] and Eighth[14] Five Year Plans. The Planning Commission has dealt with the importance of hill areas, their fragility and the factors to be considered while formulating and implementing Hill Area Development Plans.

A good profile of the Nilgiris district is available in the HADP Annual Plan[15] for 1997-98 (HADP 1997). This has been supplemented by profiles available in the Evaluation report for HADP prepared by Price Waterhouse[16] and Kurinji Project[17] prepared by Shri AMM Murugappa Chettiar Research Centre. A very detailed description of the district can be found in the Nilgiris District Gazetter published[18] in 1995.

Nilgiris district has been suffering degradation of environment since towns and estates were set up in the district in the 19th century. An interesting comparison of the present profile with that at the run of the century can be made by studying the Madras District Gazetteer of the Nilgiris district published[19] in 1908. For impressions of an earlier generation, the book "A phrenologist among the Todas", by William E Marshall[20] has been consulted.

Statistical tables about India have been taken from the statistical Outline 1995-96, published by Tata Economic Services[21]. For information about the planning strategy followed by Tamil Nadu State Government, the documents 'HADP Eight Plan Proposals[22] and HADP Annual Plan Proposals for 1994-95[23], 1995-96[24] and 1996-97[25] have been consulted[26]. In their recent evaluation report on HADP, M/s. Price WaterHouse have presented a large volume of data about HADP investments. These sources have been used to analyse HADP investments over time and by sector.

A good insight into HADP is provided by evaluation studies conducted by (a) the Institute Remote Sensing, Anna University, (b) Price WaterHouse and (c) the Department of Evaluation and Applied Research, Government of Tamil Nadu.

Macro Evaluation by Institute of Remote Sensing

Macro-evaluation of the impact of HADP on the Ecology of the Nilgiris district between the years 1983 and 1997, has been conducted by the Institute of Remote Sensing (IRS), Anna University, Chennai[27]. Since impact on ecology becomes visible only over long periods, the study covered a decade during which HADP was implemented. Remote sensing satellites make repetitive coverage of the earth's surface at regular intervals. Comparative studies of satellite imageries of the relevant periods, provide a handy tool for analyzing vegetational and land use changes. IRS carried out a multi date image analysis using IRS-IA LISS II imagery of 1997 and LANDSAT MSS imagery of 1983.

The IRS report gives taluk-wise figures of area under different land-uses between 1983 and 1997 and the changes in each taluk. The figures are summarized in the Tables 2.1 and 2.2.

TABLE - 2.1

LAND USE/LAND COVER CLASS 1983 AND 1997

Sl. No.	*Land use/Land cover*	*Area in sq. km.*		*Changes detected between 1983-1997 (sq. km.)*
		1983	*1997*	
1.	Built-up land	29.48	29.82	+ 0.34
2.	Agricultural Land			
	Crop Land	160.91	95.67	–65.24
	Fallow Land	54.04	54.04	0
	Horticulture Plantation			
	Tea, Coffee, etc.	469.13	549.81	+80.78
	Coconut, Banana, etc.	45.73	45.73	0
3.	Forest			
	Evergreen/Semi-evergreen dense	269.75	247.72	–22.03
	Fairly	101.53	123.21	+20.68
	Open	86.05	84.25	–1.80
	Deciduous Forest Dense	299.60	271.99	–57.61
	Fairly Dense	305.93	337.27	+31.34
	Open	109.50	117.49	+7.99
	Degraded forest	102.80	108.35	+5.55
	Scrub forest	67.73	57.97	–9.76
	Forest plantation	218.21	222.77	+4.56
4.	Wasteland			
	Barren rocky/stony waste			
	Sheer rock area	44.29	44.72	+0.43
	Denuded hill			
	Land with/without scrub	51.01	51.01	0
5.	Water bodies			
	Lake/Reservoir Tank	43.31	43.31	0
6.	Others			
	Grass/Grazing Land	90.00	94.72	+4.77
	Total	2,549.00	2,549.00	0

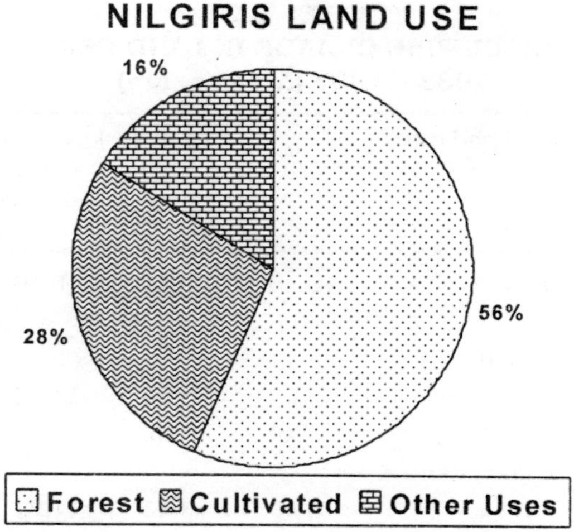

The IRS data reports decrease in agricultural area by 65 sq. km (6500 Ha) and increase in plantation area (tea + coffee) by 80 sq. km. (8000 Ha). It confirms shift from other crops to plantation crops. Since coffee area has actually declined, the increase in area under tea is more than 8000 Ha.

The changes in land use/land cover over the last decade show both enhancement as well as degradation in the vegetation status. Besides, the areas which were degraded before 1983 also continue to be in the same status.

Significant amount of conversion of lands from cultivation of vegetables or agricultural crops into horticulture plantation like Tea (Semi-perennial land cover) has been noticed by IRS.

The study of IRS also noticed decrease in vegetation status in certain areas. The study attributed this to various reasons like decrease in density of forest, conversion of forest land into horticulture plantation like tea/coffee and gradual depletion of vegetation cover.

TABLE - 2.2
TALUKWISE CHANGE IN LAND USE
1983 – 1997 (Area sq. km)

Sl. No.	*Land use/Land cover*		*Area in sq. km.* *1983*	*1997*	*Changes detected between 1983-1997 (sq. km.)*
1.	Built-up land	+0.15	+0.15	+0.10	+0.06
2.	Agricultural Land				
	Crop Land	–3.85	–3.85	–11.82	–0.56
	Fallow Land	Nil	Nil	Nil	Nil
	Horticulture Plantation				
	Tea, Coffee, etc.	+3.43	+3.43	+11.72	+14.71
3.	Forest Evergreen/Semi-				
	evergreen dense	–1.65	–1.65	–0.10	Nil
	Fairly	+0.70	+0.70	Nil	Nil
	Open	+0.75	+0.75	Nil	Nil
	Deciduous Forest Dense	–5.30	–5.30	Nil	Nil
	Fairly Dense	–1.56	–1.56	Nil	Nil
	Open	+2.69	+2.69	–2.30	–4.12
	Degraded forest	+3.00	+3.00	+1.45	Nil
	Scrub forest	+0.68	+0.68	Nil	–8.44
	Forest plantation	+0.50	+0.50	+0.85	+0.05
4.	Wasteland				
	Barren rocky/stony waste				
	Sheer rock area	+0.43	+0.43	Nil	Nil
	Denuded hill				
	Land with/without scrub	Nil	Nil	Nil	Nil
5.	Water bodies				
	Lake/Reservoir Tank	Nil	Nil	Nil	Nil
6.	Others				
	Grass/Grazing Land	+0.05	+0.05	Nil	+4.89

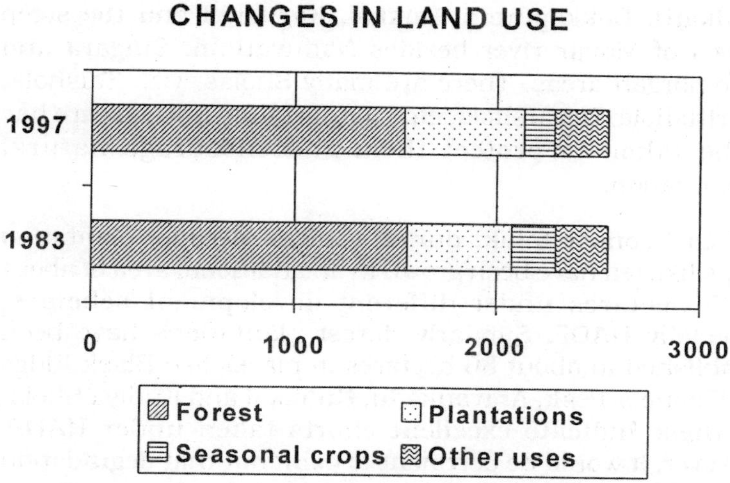

IRS has also recorded areas where poor vegetation status continues for more than ten years. The study has attributed this to various factors like acute biotic pressure on forest resources due to human and cattle population and diversion of wooded lands to non forest uses which leads to severe depletion of the cover and various types of damages like felling, encroachment, pest, diseases and damages by natural calamities like cyclone, fire, etc. This degradation continues to exist for more than ten years.

After careful analysis of the results of the study, Remote Sensing has drawn the following conclusions.

In Ootacamund taluk, the additional area brought under plantation crops like tea over the last decade is in the order of 6000 hectares extending in almost all watersheds. Forest plantations have been established in an area of about 500 hectares spread over a number of locations (not contiguous) in Nanjanad, Porthimud, Kundah, Pykara, Wenlock Down and Sigur areas. The efforts under HADP have yielded appreciable results. However, an area of about 1350 hectares is still under degraded forests mostly in Sigur and Anaikatti areas. The decrease in density of forests over about 7000 hectares needs special attention. These areas lie in Sigur,

Anaikatti, Bokkapuram, Kukkal, Kaguchhi and the steep slopes of Moyar river besides Naduvattam, Singara and Glenmorgan areas. There are many Sholas, viz., Taishola, Carrittshola, Devarshola, etc., in this taluk. Special care has to be taken to protect them and encourage natural regeneration.

In Coonoor taluk, during the last decade, plantation crops like tea have been grown in an additional area of about 1173 hectares under different development schemes, especially HADP. Similarly, forest plantations have been established in about 86 hectares in places like Black Ridge RF, Coonoor Peak, Aravankadu, Hulikkal and Kudiya Shola. All these indicate excellent efforts taken under HADP. However, it would be pertinent to point out that degradation of forest has been observed in an area of about 210 hectares especially in Bahasuramalai, Hulikkal and Nedugula, Melur Slopes and Kollakombai. The area needs immediate attention.

In Kotagiri taluk about 391 hectares have been brought under tea during the decade. About 52 hectares of forest plantations have been taken up in Kinnakorai, Nedungula, Rangaswamy Peak and the Eastern Slopes. The efforts taken under the afforestation programme are good. However, about 120 hectares are still under degraded or open conditions, especially in the eastern slopes watersheds.

In Gudalur taluk, additional area of about 1500 hectares has been brought under plantation crop like tea during the decade under study. While an area of about 50 hectares has been covered under forest plantations, still around 500 hectares and more are under degraded conditions.

Summarizing, the IRS has observed that commendable efforts have been taken up under a variety of programmes, especially HADP to restore the ecology of this hill district. The efforts taken in this regard have helped in checking degradation of this area. IRS has suggested that a crash programme would be needed to ensure afforestation in contiguous areas over a five year period in areas where degradation is highly pronounced as indicated in its report.

The study emphasizes that special programmes would be needed in Sigur, Anaikatti, Eastern Slopes, Geddai and Bokkapuram areas.

Evaluation Studies by Price Waterhouse

Evaluation of major HADP schemes was first done by Price Waterhouse in the year 1986. By then, HADP was already in operation for 12 years. Price Waterhouse made another evaluation of major sectors of HADP in their report of 1997. The report[27] has the following general observations:

Market demand based activities like tea, soil conservation and engineering measures have been emphasized without due consideration for ecological balance. Priorities are based on very limited understanding of environmental issues and Nilgiris ecological system. The focus of the efforts seems to be only on degraded watersheds (as priorities are based on levels of soil erosion as measured by the soil erosion index). This results in focusing only on one dimension of the environmental issues. It is imperative to note that soil erosion is the ultimate result of the entire process of degradation. It may be desirable to focus on prevention rather than treating the disease. The remaining ecologically critical but fragile system assumes greater importance in this context. Significant proportion of funds are utilized for developing departmental infrastructure. There is limited participation of people in the development efforts. Projects are selected and executed through departments/ contractors with low involvement of people in the process. Schemes have concentrated only on traditional activities like tea, pulp wood, engineering solution to soil erosion, etc. The economic and environmental changes and developments in science and technology are not fully reflected in the scheme design and delivery. Resources are concentrated on tea promotion as both horticulture and Soil conservation department's main activities are in this area (about 40 per cent of HADP funds are annually allocated to these two sectors). The "mindset" of implementing officials and their departmental approach curtails innovative solutions.

After a critical examination of the schemes of Horticulture Department for promoting Tea, the Price Waterhouse study makes the following observations:

1. Broad allocations for the schemes – production and planting programmes – make it difficult to analyze the efficacy of the implementation programme. Analysis based on available data indicates that the cost effectiveness of the programme has deteriorated. The cost of production has increased from Rs. 1.05 to Rs. 3.34 per VP Clone during 1991 and 1993. Market price of tea clones from private small nursery during this period was ranging from Re. 0.50 – 1.00 per clone.

2. The coverage of the programme has been thinly spread over 70 identified micro watersheds. However, the concentration of efforts seems to have been in Ooty taluk. About 15 per cent of the efforts are in the Nanjanad watershed. UPASI's pilot testing indicates that the watersheds like Nanjanad – which have higher elevation with frost – are not suitable for tea cultivation.

3. The scheme has been concentrating on area expansion rather than improving the productivity of the existing areas. The infilling programme has been stopped to "discipline the small farmers". A low bush density negates the rationality on which the scheme has been built upon – a green cover to prevent soil erosion and increased income for small farmers.

4. Slope levels for tea conversion have not been strictly adhered to. Price Waterhouse survey indicates about 30 per cent of the converted lands are used for other purposes.

5. The fact that about 70 per cent of annual crop land was converted to tea may be considered as a positive achievement towards the stated objectives.

6. On an average HADP funds are utilized to develop about 500 hectares of tea every year. The share of HADP in new area development works out to about 25 per cent, as on an average about Two thousand hectares of land per annum were developed into tea in the last decade. Thus the demand and income driven by the market forces seem to have a greater impact on the decisions of the farmers. The offer price of Horticulture department after subsidy is more or less equivalent to the prevailing market price for the clones. The efficiency of small private nurseries often managed by unemployed youth provides the basis for this competitive pricing. Thus in the present system there are sufficient arrangements for continuous supply of clones. However, any reduction of subsidized clones supply from HADP is expected to push the market price of clones. In an indirect manner this may act as a deterrent to speedier growth of tea areas.

Price Waterhouse has conducted a survey to assess the relative significance of various factors responsible for the growth of tea area in Nilgiris district. The results of Price Waterhouse survey are summarized in Table 2.3 below:

TABLE - 2.3

FACTORS BEHIND GROWTH OF TEA AREA

Sl. No.	*Reasons for Diversification*	*Level of influence*
1	Incidence of pests, diseases and low productivity	60
2	Soil erosion in lands	10
3	Rising cost of Annual crop cultivation	40
4	Uncertainty of potato revenue	65
5	Attractive Tea pricing	25
6	Regularity of income from Tea	90
7	Subsidy for Tea	20

Source: Price Waterhouse, (1997), Evaluation of HADP – Final Report

The above survey results indicate that subsidy under HADP programme is only a facilitator for the conversion process rather than the determining factor. A host of factors such as attractive price for tea and collapse of annual crop economy seems to be the dominant reasons for conversion. The fact that more than 75 per cent of the conversion is without HADP assistance substantiates the factors behind the conversion.

The crop diversification scheme implemented by UPASI with the support of Tea Board since 1981 has also supplied about four lakhs tea clones per annum, free of cost to as many growers as possible, subject to a maximum of 5000 clones per grower. Price Waterhouse report states that their discussions with officials of Tea industry/UPASI indicates that in their perception, significant scope is still available for expanding the tea area in the Nilgiris. The existence of about 275 private nurseries with an estimated capacity of 25 million tea clones per annum indicates the market expectations on the tea growth.

The critics of the unplanned growth of tea in Nilgiris say that the Blue Mountain is getting converted into a "green desert". On the other hand, the Horticulture department and Tea industry sources equate tea plantation with tree cover. Price Waterhouse has examined certain key issues for balanced growth of tea.

- Tea bushes are estimated to have only 40 years productive (optimum yield) life. The age yield profile of the tea bush indicates that the yield per bush reaches a peak at somewhere around 20 to 30 years.

- The canopy density of tea plantation is not comparable to that of forest cover. During the initial 4 years after planting and after periodic pruning the land is as exposed as any other cultivated area.

- The Forestry Act as well as internationally accepted best practices require that slope levels above 33 per cent should be left with forest/tree cover. This is to prevent human interventions in any form in the environmentally sensitive areas. In Nilgiris this basic rule has not been adhered to.

- Tea plantations are better than annual crop lands in controlling soil erosion only when managed well. However, given the structure of the tea industry with a very large number of small holdings, a significant portion of the area is very poorly managed. The Geological Survey of India study on incidence of land slides in Nilgiris focused on this issue. Table 2.4 summarizes the Geological Survey of India findings.

- For ensuring the eco-relevance of tea, regulation of plantation on slopes and scientific farm management practices need to be enforced.

Price Waterhouse found the implementation of forestry schemes generally satisfactory in the work-spots visited. Roadside avenue planting was successful and pleasing with Pinus patula, doing very well.

TABLE - 2.4
INCIDENCE OF LANDSLIDES Vs. LAND USE IN NILGIRIS

Land use Practice	*Percentage of Land slides*
Potato and Vegetables	34.23
Tea and Coffee	34.23
Open Dense Forest	11.16
Built up Areas	9.45
Forest Plantation	5.85
Roads and Railways	2.25
Water Bodies	1.80

Source: Price Waterhouse, (1997), Evaluation of HADP – Final Report

The delineation of Reserved Forest boundaries and the erection of cairns has led to the detection of many encroachments over valuable forest land by neighbouring estate owners and the resumption of the encroached land. The creation of firewood depots has meant that the poorer sections of the people can obtain at least a part of their requirements of a daily necessity at reasonable rates. The introduction of wattle in bluegum plantations and the fostering of natural regeneration of wattle in felled wattle plantations offer the most promising indications of a technique for general adoption to reclothe denuded areas. In the plateau, nature needs but very little assistance to heal the ghastly scars left by cultivation of annual crops or tea on steep slopes or mismanagement due to other causes. Fresh wattle seed available on the ground (from natural seed fall or from organized distribution in treeless gaps), a light burn to dispose of the slash and stimulate the seed at the proper time before the pre-monsoon showers and a dense mass of wattle regeneration takes possession of the ground after the monsoon.

- Chain link fencing has given new life to the sholas. Though costly, yet the results in terms of the new natural regeneration of valuable species are impressive. However, this proliferation of chain link fences underlines our general failure to use un-reserves and patta lands to create firewood plantations to act as a buffer and a bulwark against destruction of sholas to meet firewood needs.

- The Genepool garden at Kodanad is situated in the comparatively drier part of the Nilgiris, receiving only the North East monsoon. The sholas are less imposing and dense but are nevertheless valuable as genepools. Price Waterhouse has endorsed the following comments:

- Though much is talked about the shola forests, the natural regeneration of the constituent species is not well understood. Therefore, this aspect needs detailed study.

- As far as the propagation is concerned, it will be worthwhile to construct low cost mist chambers for studying the vegetative propagation of species.

- Multiplication of the rare, endangered, threatened and endemic species, their reintroduction in ideal natural habitat and studies on their establishment are to be carried out.

- Selected shola species multiplied may be planted in degraded sholas available elsewhere, for their eco-restoration.

- Ethno-botanical surveys have already been carried out among the Todas by Bharathiar University and the findings of these surveys may be useful to chalk out future research programme. Detailed surveys and studies, especially on the etheno-pharmacology, among local ethnic communities may bring out a lot of new information.

- The phytographical importance of the Nilgiris, where the Western Ghats and Eastern Ghats meet is well understood, but the efforts taken to conserve the bio-diversity is inadequate. In this context, the research activities proposed in the Genepool reserve for Southern Montane Wet Temperate Forests at Kodanad will go a long way in conserving the ecological and genetic diversity of the area. Restriction of annual cultivation to slopes less than 1 in 10 and permanent tree cover for slopes steeper than 1 in 3 continue to be disregarded axioms. The need to set apart distinct areas for afforestation for protective functions, commercial forestry and social forestry is still inadequately realized. The role of social forestry in the Nilgiris is as yet marginal, the current annual planting target being only 40 HA.

Micro Evaluation by DEAR

Concurrent evaluation by the Department of Evaluation and Applied Research (DEAR) is built into HADP. A Cell for this purpose is supported in that department through HADP funds. The DEAR has evaluated the following schemes so far:

(a) Scheme for Sanctuary for rosewood and its Associates[28].

(b) Schemes for providing assistance to Tea with special reference to modernization of Tea factories.[29]

(c) Schemes for Rural Water Supply.[30]

(d) Artificial Insemination scheme.[31]

(e) Frozen semen production scheme.[32]

(f) Welfare of SC and ST.[33]

Of the above, the reports on Tea Assisted schemes conducted in 1990 and 1995, are very relevant to the present study.

Others

The Tamil Nadu Agricultural University has conducted 'An Evaluation study on the impact of Small Tea Growers' Development Schemes of the Tea Board in South India'. This report[34] contains detailed discussion of the schemes of Tea Board and reports based on survey of beneficiaries. A large volume of statistical data about Tea cultivation in India is available in the publication "Tea Statistics 1993-94" of the Tea Board.[35] A history of tea cultivation in the Nilgiris can be seen in the book of Muthiah S.[36] which examines the history of tea cultivation in the Nilgiris.

Madhav Gadgil and Ramachandra Guha[37] (1993) discuss the role of Government Policy in the last hundred years in the destruction of forests in the country. A discussion of US

National Parks Policy may be seen in Anderson and Leal[38] (1990).

The Central Soil and Water Conservation Research and Training Institute, Ooty has conducted a number of studies related to soil loss and soil conservation in the Nilgiris District[39 to 42]. This Institute is studying soil and water conservation in the Nilgiris since 1975.

The Geological Survey of India has been monitoring land-slides in the Nilgiris. Useful data is found in Ramachandran, KP[43] on the land slide inventory in Nilgiris district.

A critical study of the tea industry in India may be seen in 'The Indian Tea Industry', by ICRA.[44]

Publications of UPASI[45], Coonoor provide the Planters' view point regarding extension of Tea area in the Nilgiris.[46]

Views of a local environment group are seen in 'Intensive Environmental Education – a pilot project' of the 'Save Nilgiris Campaign'[47].

Much data about INCOSERVE[48], a federation of industrial tea cooperatives in the Nilgiris has been obtained from a note received from INCOSERVE.

The Tea Board has a regional office in Coonoor. This office also assists farmers willing to shift to tea cultivation. Roy Chaudhary (1997)[49] provides useful data about such schemes of the Tea Board.

A note from TANTEA[50] details the activities of the Tamil Nadu Tea Plantations Limited, a Corporation floated by the Tamil Nadu Forest Department. The Corporation is growing tea on erstwhile forest lands.

Notes were collected from the Geo-technical Cell[51], the Agro-Engineering Department, the Horticultural Department, the Forest Department and the HADP Cell.

While a wide range of reference material has been consulted, the researcher has not come across any work similar to the present research study on quantifying the role of HADP in promoting tea cultivation. Hence, this study may be regarded, as a study of a specific aspect not researched earlier.

References

1. WCED (1987), 'Our Common Future' (World Commission on Environment and Development), Oxford University Press, New York.

2. Chattopadhyay Srikumar (1995) Environment and Development (Views from the East and the West), Ed. Mukherjee A and Agnihotri VK, Concept Publishing Co., New Delhi 59, pp. 39-47.

3. Blowers Andrew (1995) Environment and Development, *op. cit.* pp. 349-359.

4. Dasgupta Partha, Carl Fonke and Karle Goran Maler (1994) Population, Economic Development and the Environment, Ed. Kiessling KL and Landberg H, Oxford University Press, New York, pp. 164-180

5. Rao, UR (1995), Statistical Dynamics of Sustainable Development, Man and Development, Vol. XVII, No.2, *Industrial Development*, pp. 1-7.

6. Gohlert Ernest (1993), Foundation of Sustainable Development, Proceedings of the International Conference on Sustainable Village Based Development, Colorado State University, Fort Coliins, USA, pp. 105-138.

7. Pranesh, MB (1993), 'Sustainable Village Based Development – Central Government Policy – The Indian

Picture', Proceedings of the International Conference on Sustainable Village Based Development, Op Cit. pp. 505-538.

8. Banskota. M and Pratap. T. (1996) 'Education, Research and Sustainable Mountain Agriculture', International Centre for Integrated Mountain Development', Kathmandu, pp. 1-32.

9. International Food Policy Research Institute and the National Geographic Society (1995), A 2020 Vision for Food and Environment, Washington, DC.

10. Sachs Ignacy (1995), 'Searching for new development strategies – challenges of the Social Summit', *Economic and Political Weekly*, June 8, pp. 1682-91.

11. Chand Ramesh (1996), 'Ecological and economic impact of horticultural development in the Himalayas' *Economic and Political Weekly*, June 29, pp. 493-99.

12. Government of India(1980), Planning Commission, *Sixth Five Year Plan* 1980-85, pp. 413-415.

13. Government of India (1985), Planning Commission, *Seventh Five Year Plan* 1985-90, Vol.II, pp. 338-343.

14. Government of India(1992), Planning Commission, *Eighth Five Year Plan* 1992-97, Vol.II, pp. 426-438.

15. Government of Tamil Nadu (1992), Planning and Development Department, HADP Eighth Plan Proposals, 1992-97.

16. Price Waterhouse (1997), *HADP Evaluation Final Report*, Price Waterhouse, 610, Anna Salai, Chennai – 600 006.

17. MCRC (1970), *Project Kurinji – Nilgiris Integrated Energy Perspective*, Shri AMM Murugappa Chettiar Research Centre, Chennai-113.

18. Government of Tamil Nadu (1975), Gazetteers of India, Tamil Nadu State. The Nilgiris district Ed. M Gopalakrishnan.

19. Francis.W (1908), Madras District Gazetteer of the Nilgiris District, Government of Tamil Nadu reprinted 1994 by Asian Educational Services, New Delhi-16.

20. Marshall WE (1873), A phrenologist among the Todas, Longmans and Green, London reprinted 1995 by Asian Educational Services, New Delhi.16.

21. Tata Services Ltd., (1995), 'Statistical Outline of India 1995-96', Department of Economics and Statistics, Tata Services Ltd., Mumbai-1.

22. Government of Tamil Nadu (1994), Statistical Handbook of Tamil Nadu, Department of Statistics, Chennai-6.

23. Government of Tamil Nadu (1994), (2), Planning and Development Department, *HADP Annual Plan proposals 1994-95*.

24. Government of Tamil Nadu (1995), (2b), Planning and Development Department, *HADP Annual Plan proposals 1995-96*.

25. Government of Tamil Nadu (1995), (3), Planning and Development Department, *HADP Integrated Watershed Development Plan 1995-96*.

26. Government of Tamil Nadu (1996), Planning and Development Department, *HADP Annual Plan proposals 1996-97*.

27. Anna University (1996), Institute of Remote Sensing, *Macro-evaluation of the impact of HADP on the ecology of the Nilgiris district between the years 1983 and 1994*, Anna University, Chennai.

28. Tamil Nadu Agricultural University (1996), Department of Agro-economics, *An Evaluation Study on the Impact of Small Tea Growers*, Development schemes of the Tea Board in South India', TNAU, Coimbatore.

29. Tea Board (1993), Tea Statistics 1993-94, Tea Board, Calcutta.

30. Muthiah.S. (1993), A Planting Century, The first hundred years of UPASI, Affiliated East West Press, Chennai-10.

31. Government of Tamil Nadu (1992), Department of Evaluation and Applied Research', *Evaluation Study on Sanctuary for Rosewood and its associates under HADP.*

32. Government of Tamil Nadu (1995), (4), Department of Evaluation and Applied Research, *'A repeat study on schemes providing assistance to tea with special reference to modernization of tea factories under HADP'.*

33. Government of Tamil Nadu (1995), (5), Department of Evaluation and Applied Research, *'Evaluation Study on Rural Water Supply under HADP'.*

34. Government of Tamil Nadu (1995), (2), Department of Evaluation and Applied Research, *'Evaluation of Artificial Insemination scheme under HADP'.*

35. Government of Tamil Nadu (1996), (2), Department of Evaluation and Applied Research, *'Evaluation of frozen semen production scheme under HADP'.*

36. Government of Tamil Nadu (1996), (2), Department of Evaluation and Applied Research, *'Evaluation of schemes for Welfare of SC and ST under HADP'.*

37. Gadgil Madhav and Guha Ramachandra (1993), This Fissured Land, an ecological history of India, Oxford University Press, Delhi.

38. Anderson Terry and Leal DR (1990), Free Market Environmentalism, Pacific Research Institute for Public Policy, San Francisco.

39. Central Soil and Water Conservation Research and Training Institute (1972), *'Package of practices for Soil and Water Conservation in the Nilgiris region'*, CSWCRTI, Ootacamund.

40. Central Soil and Water Conservation Research and Training Institute (1980), Rainfall frequency Atlas of the Nilgiris, CSWCRTI, Ootacamund.

41. Central Soil and Water Conservation Research and Training Institute (1982), *Soil and Water Conservation in Hill region of India*, Proceedings of working group, CSWCRTI, Ootacamund.

42. Central Soil and Water Conservation Research and Training Institute (1987), *Effect of blue gum plantation on water yield in the Nilgiris*, CSWCRTI, Ootacamund.

43. Geological Survey of India (1996), *'A report on the land slide inventory in Nilgiris district'* by Ramachandran, KP, GSI, Chennai.

44. ICRA Investment Information Publication (1996), The Indian Tea Industry, ICRA Industry Watch Services No.2, ICRA Ltd., New Delhi-2.

45. United Planters' Association of South India (1995), *The Planters Voice*, September 1995, UPASI, Coonoor.

46. United Planters' Association of South India (1997), *Importance of Plantation Crops in South India*, UPASI, Coonoor

47. Save Nilgiris Campaign (1990), *Intensive Environmental Education – A pilot project, Save Nilgiris Campaign*, Ootacamund.

48. INCOSERVE (1999), *Short notes on the performance of Industrial Co-operative Tea factories and INCOSERVE in the Nilgiris district*, INCOSERVE, Coonoor

49. Roy Choudhury. A. (1997), *A note of Tea Board Financial assistance schemes for the Development of Small tea growers in South India*, Tea Board Regional Office, Coonoor.

50. TANTEA (1999), *A note on the activities of the Tamil Nadu Tea Plantations Ltd.*, TANTEA, Coonoor.

51. Government of Tamil Nadu (1997), Department of Geology, Geo-Technical Cell, *Note on land slides in the Nilgiris.*

Beneficial Effects of Crop Diversification

In the hill areas, agriculture is the key sector for employment and income generation because large scale industrialisation is not ecologically desirable and the infrastructure is too poor to attract industries. Traditional crops have low income potential. Hence emphasis has been laid on promotion of horticultural crops. There is also the requirement of packing material for marketing horticultural produce which has led to damage to forests. However, detailed studies have shown that the adverse effects are not considerable. Demand for packing cases is no longer met by cutting timber from forests [illegible]. Diversification to horticultural crops has resulted in positive effects like reduction in crop intensity, soil erosion, livestock pressure and grazing incidence and improvement in income. It has also had favourable ecological implications. Forests in the vicinity of economically improved villages suffer less damage than forests near economically backward villages. Low income and poverty are the major forces of over-exploitation of natural resources. Improvement in socio-economic conditions brought about by diversion to horticultural crops benefits people as well as ecology.

Cultivation of Tea

In particular, diversification of cultivation from cereal crops to cultivation of tea, aids sustainable development of hill areas. Annual tilling causes loss of valuable top soil where annual crops are cultivated. This causes irreparable damage to the farmers by loss of fertility of the soil. It also reduces the storage capacity of hydro electric and irrigation reservoirs located in the foot hills. If the crop is substituted by tea, water loss can be greatly reduced. There is also tremendous improvement in the economic condition of small farmers due to increase in their income from annual crops to tea. This has resulted in improvement of living conditions. The promotion of tea plantation has not only helped in the conservation of the hills, but also brought about economic improvement of farming community.

3

Profile of the Nilgiris District

The word Nilgiris (once spelt Nilagiris or Neilgherries) is derived from two Sanskrit words: "nilam" meaning blue and "giri" meaning a hill. Thus the literal meaning is, "The Blue Hills". When it was named so, is not clear. However the origin of the name is at once apparent to anybody who has, from a distance, viewed the Hills, rising majestically enveloped in a peculiar blue haze which usually shrouds them. The Nilgiris District forms an integral part of the Western Ghats. It has an area of 2549 sq. km. located between 11 degrees 10' and 11 degrees 45' N latitude and 76 degrees 14' and 77 degree 02' E longitude. It is bounded on the north by Karnataka State, north-west by Kerala State, south-east by Coimbatore District and north-east by Erode District of Tamil Nadu[1].

Administrative Setup

For the purpose of administration, the district has been divided into four blocks viz., Udhagamandalam, Coonoor, Kothagiri and Gudalur, with the District Headquarters at Udhagamandalam (Ooty). The district is divided into two revenue divisions and six taluks. (Till recently, the district had only four taluks viz., Ooty, Coonoor, Kothagiri and Gudalur. The taluks of Kundah and Pandalur have been formed recently by bifurcating Ooty and Gudalur taluks). For local administration, the district has two Municipalities, one Cantonment, four Panchayat Unions, twenty one Town Panchayats and twenty seven village Panchayats.

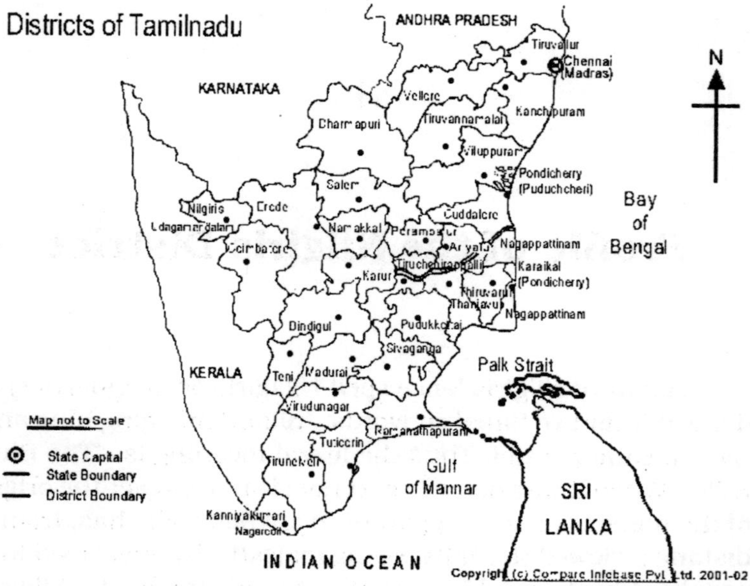

Division based on Physical Features

On the basis of geology, topography, climate and nature of vegetation, the district can be divided into five sub-regions[2].

Gudalur Plateau: This region covers parts of Gudalur and Ooty taluks. This region constitutes an extension of the plateau of Kerala State. The maximum height (2222 m) is noticed at Naduvattam town and the minimum height (962 m) is found at Nelliyalam town. However the average height of this region is around 1200 to 1300 m.

Mudumalai Forested hills: This small region lies in the northern tip of this district, covering a portion of Gudalur taluk. This region consists of the well known Mudumalai forest, with a wildlife sanctuary mainly of elephants. Both the maximum height (1136 m) and minimum height (900 m) of the region are in the Mudumalai forest village. From this area, the tributaries of the Moyar river originate.

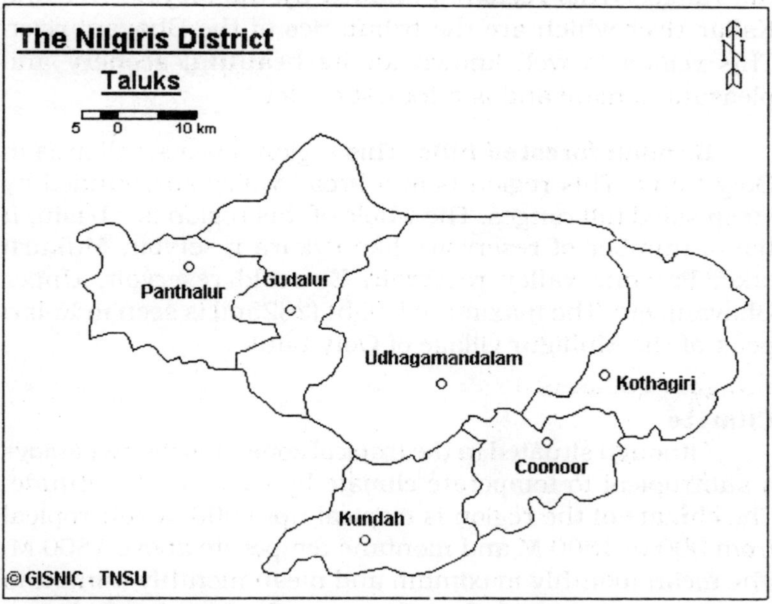

Sigur forested hills: This region lies in the northern portion of the district, comprising parts of Ooty and Kothagiri taluks. This region is the meeting point of western and eastern ghats. The maximum height (1764 m) is found at Ebbanad village of Kothagiri taluk and the minimum height (665 m) is in the forest area. This region slopes from west towards east. It forms the catchment area of Moyar river.

Ooty Plateau: This region has comparatively larger area of the district comprising the whole of Coonoor Taluk and parts of the taluks of Ooty and Kothagiri. This region lies at the meeting point of western and eastern Ghats. Doddabetta (2644 m) the highest peak of the State is located here. Average altitude in this plateau is 2100 to 2200 m. The steep hills and narrow valleys with numerous rivers and rivulets running in all directions with a few waterfalls at some places provide beautiful scenery. The minimum height seen in this region is (1618m) at Kilkundah Village of Ooty taluk. This whole region lies in the valley and it is surrounded by steep sloping hill ranges. This region is drained by the Moyar river and Kallar river which are the tributaries of the Bhavani river. This region is well known for its beautiful scenery and pleasant climate and is a tourist center.

Kundah forested hills: This region has a small area in Ooty taluk. This region is in a broad valley surrounded by steep sided hill ranges. The whole of this region is a basin. It has a number of reservoirs like Pykara reservoir, Mukurti lake, Parsons valley reservoir, Emerald reservoir, Upper Bhavani, etc. The maximum height (2625m) is seen in Kolari peak of the Mulligur village of Ooty taluk .

Climate

Although situated in the tropical zone, this district enjoys a subtropical to temperate climate by virtue of its altitude. The climate of the region is tropical upto 900 M subtropical from 900 to 1800 M and montane temperate above 1800 M. The mean monthly maximum and mean monthly minimum temperatures recorded at Ooty are 22.1 and 8.5 degree centigrade occurring in the months of April and January respectively. No snow occurs in this region. South-west monsoon occurs from June to August and North-East monsoon from September to December. The coldest month is December and the hottest month is April during which a dry wind blows from the north-east. Frosty nights are common during January and February. Wind velocity of this region shows maximum and minimum of 13.4 Km/hr and 4.4 Km/hr respectively. Mean monthly humidity also ranges from 70 per cent in December to 94 per cent in July[3].

Rainfall

Average rainfall in the district is 1180 mm (average of 1960-94). Highest rainfall of 3000 mm has been recorded at Devala in Gudalur taluk. The first three months of the year are almost rainless. February is found to be the driest month. Rainfall is spread over all the four seasons of the year viz., December - March, April – May, June – August and September

– November, with most of the rainfall concentrated during June through November. Maximum amount of rainfall is recorded during July – 299.5 mm. Intense rainfall often occurs in the months of October, July, May and November respectively, in that order. Erosion intensity is high in May, October and July. The incidence of drought is also common in Nilgiris. From soil and water conservation point of view, high incidence of drought during April and December and heavy rainfall during October, July and May are of significance.

Geology

Geology of the Deccan Plateau indicates that the area is very stable compared to Northern Plains and Himalayas. The geology of the area consists of charnockites of Nilgiri gneiss varying from acid to ultra basic ones. The intermediate synordite are the most common geological formations. The minerals present in the rock are blue quartz, plagioclass feldspars, hornblenders and secondary minerals such as garnets etc.

Soils

The soils of the Nilgiris are lateritic in origin with shallow to deep soil. The soils are porous but the infiltration is not so high as to cope with the high intensities of rainfall that occur sometimes. This results in the formation of surface runoff that scours not only the fertile top soil but also washes down the applied fertilizers and manures from the cultivated fields. The soils are acidic (PH 4.6 to 6.1) and are generally deficient in plant nutrients. However, even the most leached and badly eroded soils have the capacity to recuperate rapidly by proper application of organic and inorganic manures and fertilizers.

Biodiversity

Nilgiris district harbours a wonderful collection of flora and fauna. Considering the richness of biological diversity in the district, the area was chosen in 1986 as the site for conservation of biological diversity of peninsular India and was designated as the Nilgiris Biosphere Reserve (NBR) and UNESCO "Man and the Biosphere" Programme of the Department of Environment and Forest, Government of India.

The natural vegetation of the valley is typically a dense rather low forest with much undergrowth and many epiphytes, mosses and ferns. Both tropical and temperate flora occur, vegetation being mostly tropical in character at lower elevations and temperate at higher elevations. Botanically as well as zoologically and ethnologically, the Nilgiris forms a distinct ecological realm of its own. The typical forests of Nilgiris are called as "Sholas". The different types of vegetation met with are:

1. The Shola and grassland vegetation of the Nilgiris plateau.
2. The open sandal bearing scrub of the Sigur plateau.
3. The moist deciduous and the dry deciduous teak forest of the Nilgiris–Wynad and
4. The forest of south-eastern outer slopes.

Forests

Forest area varies from about 22 per cent in Coonoor taluk to 66 per cent in Ooty taluk with an average of 56.6 per cent for the Nilgiris District. Man-made forests comprise of Eucalyptus globulus (96.6 sq. km.), E.Grandia (37.2 sq. km.), E.citridora (0. 8 sq. km.), Acacia mearnsil (140.8 sq. km.), Pinus patula (11.9 sq. km.). Natural forests called "Shola" occupy a meager area of 15 sq. km. The district has been attracting the attention of ecologists for a long time, because of two distinct plant communities, viz., extensive grasslands and evergreen "Shola". Trees in the shola belong to the families of Bricaceae, Lauranceae, Myrtaceae, Rosaceae and Styraceae represented by genera like Litsea, Phoebe, Rhododendron, Siderroxylon, Syzgium, etc. The sholas have top storey, under storey, undergrowth, dense leaf litter and humus along with good growth of epiphytes, lichens, mosses and lianes. A good number of perennial streams originate from these "Sholas". A botanical study of the "Shola" has revealed that no single species predominates. The "Shola" adds greatly to the beauty of the country side; and is of immense use in protecting the perennial sources of water supply in the streams and for the general maintenance of ecological balance.

Flora

Out of the 141 endemic genera in India, 50 are spread over Western Ghats and 11 in Nilgiris. At the species level, out of the estimated 2100 species of flowering plants endemic to peninsular India, 818 are to be found in the Nilgiris and adjoining areas. The genus Baeolepis with a single species nervosa is restricted to the Nilgiris. Of the 168 species of endangered flowering plants of Tamil Nadu, 25 are exclusive to the Nilgiris and include many orchids. A large number of medicinal plants occur here. About 200 species have been reported, of which 24 are commercially exploited. Due to over exploitation certain species have become rare.

Fauna

Very little information is available about the invertebrates excepting butterflies. The best known animals are however the vertebrates, especially the larger mammals. There are already efforts towards the protection of endangered and endemic mammals such as Asian Elephant, tiger, Nilgiri tahr, Nilgiris langur, Nilgiri marten, etc. Over 300 species of birds are known, of which 15 are endemic to western ghats and Nilgiris. Laughing thrush is exclusive to the higher hills of Nilgiris. The Nilgiri wood pigeon listed as globally endangered, is found frequently within the Nilgiri Biospheric reserve.

Demography

The total population of Nilgiris District is 7.48 lakhs as per 1991 census, forming 1.3 percent of total population of Tamil Nadu. The population of this district has registered a decadal growth rate of 11.84 per cent from 1981 to 1991. The distribution of male and female population with rural and urban character is given in Table 3.1.

TABLE - 3.1
NILGIRIS DISTRICT POPULATION – 1991

	Population	*Rural*	*Urban*
Male	358129	178910	179219
Female	352085	177874	174211
Total	710214	356784	353430

Source: Govt. of Tamil Nadu 1994, Pocket Book of Statistics p-10.

Rural population is 50.24 per cent of the total population as compared to the State average of 65.85 per cent. The degree of urbanization of this hilly district (49.76 per cent) is higher than the State average of 34.15 per cent.

Total scheduled caste population is 214598, representing 30.3 per cent of the population. The Scheduled Tribe population is 25048, representing 4 per cent of the total district population. These figures are higher than the State average figures of 19.19 per cent and 1.03 per cent respectively. The Scheduled Caste population is distributed equally in rural and semi-urban areas, whereas three fourth of the Scheduled Tribes are living in rural areas. Todas, Kothas, Kurumbas, Paniyas and Irulas are the important tribes in the Nilgiris District.

The density of the population is 279.5 per sq. km as against the density of population of 420 per sq. km. for the State. Taluk-wise figures can be seen in Table 3.2.

TABLE - 3.2
TALUK-WISE DENSITY OF POPULATION - 1991

Sl. No.	*Taluks*	*Area*	*Population %*	*1991*	*Percen-tage*	*Density/ Person/ Sq.Km*
1.	Ooty	1197.63	47.10	238578	34.6	199.21
2.	Coonoor	228.03	9.00	177155	25.0	776.87
3.	Kothagiri	396.65	15.60	113686	16.0	286.62
4.	Gudalur	718.24	28.30	180795	24.4	251.72

Source: HADP Cell, 1997, 'HADP, An Approach Paper', P.5.

Although Ooty Taluk accounts for 34.6 per cent of the total population of the district, the density of population is very low compared to other taluks. The density of population is very high in Coonoor followed by Kothagiri.

The level of literacy is 71.7 per cent which is higher than the State average of 62.7 per cent probably because of higher urban population in the district. The level of literacy among men is 57.2 per cent while it is 42.8 per cent among females[5].

Land Holding Pattern

The holding size is small in the district, averaging 1.94 Ha. Roughly 78 per cent of the holdings are less than 1 Ha each in size.

The pattern of land-holding is highly skewed with less than 13 per cent of the area being shared by over 20000 small holdings while 45 per cent of the area is enjoyed by 106 large holdings. If a small farmer is defined as one having upto 2 Ha. of land, the district has nearly 27000 small farmers sharing among themselves 25 per cent of the area, distributed over 87 per cent of the operational holdings. The skewed pattern of land holding is dictated by the district's cropping pattern, dominated by plantation crops. The land use pattern may be seen in Table 3.3.

In Nilgiris District, there is good change in the cropping pattern after Hill Area Development Programme was introduced. The main emphasis under Hill Area Development Programme is to increase the perennial crops to reduce the soil erosion problem and increase the vegetation cover for eco-development.

TABLE - 3.3
LANDUSE PATTERN

	Ha.	*Percentage of total Area*
A. Total Geographical Area	254381	(100)
B. i) Forest	143359	(56.3)
ii) Barren and Uncultivable land	2712	(1.1)
iii) Land put to non-agricultural use	8752	(3.4)
iv) Cultivable Waste	2875	(1.1)
v) Permanent pastures and other grazing land	4718	(1.9)
vi) Miscellaneous tree crops and groves (not included in the net area sown)	2206	(0.9)
vii) Current fallow lands	11683	(4.6)
viii) Other fallow lands	7722	(3.0)
ix) Net area sown	70354	(27.7)
C. Area sown more than once	1305	(0.5)
D. Gross cropped area (GCA)	71659	(28.2)

Source: HADP Cell, 1997, 'HADP – An Approach Paper, P-9'

Land Cover

Land in the Nilgiris was covered with "shola" (Southern Wet Montane temperate evergreen forests) with rolling grasslands. Todas, the original tribals who were pastoral in habit burnt the forests and brought them under grass. Yet an equilibrium was maintained. Later, Badagas arrived and started cultivation. British settles introduced potato, tea, eucalyptus, acacia and temperate fruit trees in the 19th century. Natural forests and grasslands gave way to extensive cultivation of tea, coffee, cinchona, bluegum, black wattle, peaches, pears, plums, oranges, potato, temperate vegetables etc. Out of these induced changes, maximum change and havoc was created by tea, coffee, potato and vegetable crops without adoption of suitable conservation measures, with the result, ill managed potato, tea, vegetable crops, etc. not only produced heavy soil loss and run off but also spoiled the mountain landscape and beauty of the region. Tea, paddy, tapioca, banana, ginger, turmeric etc., have been introduced at Gudalur and Pandalur causing heavy erosion .

Agriculture

Of the total area of the district, only one fourth is cultivated. Non-food crops are cultivated in nearly 65 per cent of the area and food crops in the balance 35 per cent. Tea and Coffee are major non-food crops grown. Tea is grown in over 50 per cent of the total area which is mainly located in Ooty, Coonoor and Kothagiri. Next is Coffee, which is grown in nearly 2,000 hectares mainly in Gudalur. Cinchona and lemon grass are the other major non-food crops grown.

Among the food crops, potato is grown in a large scale. Paddy and cereals are grown in Gudalur area, which has the only terrain suitable for this type of cultivation. Potato, Carrot, Beans, Beetroot, Radish, Cauliflower are the major vegetables grown in this district. As per the recent survey, vegetables are grown in over 7,500 hectares of the total cultivated area. Bulk of the vegetables grown in Nilgiris are transported to other centers in the State for sale.

Fruits are also grown in this district on a limited scale. The area under fruit crops is 612 hectares as per the recent survey. Orange, Jack fruits, Plums, Peaches, Bananas, Pears, Apples and Mangoes are the fruits grown in a limited scale in Nilgiris District. Plums of Udhagamandalam area and mandarin oranges of the Kookal valley of Udhagamandalam block are the well known varieties grown here. The horticulture department is actively engaged in popularizing fruits cultivation.

Ginger, cardamom, lemon grass, garlic. rubber, cinchona and pepper are also grown in a limited scale in Gudalur block. Eucalyptus and Geranium are grown substantially in Udhagamandalam block. There are a number of Eucalyptus oil and Geranium oil extracting units functioning in this area. The extracted Eucalyptus oil and Geranium oil are sold throughout the country.

Industry

The main industry of the Nilgiris District is processing of Tea. There are about 185 Tea Factories spread throughout the district. The Coffee produced in the district is cured either at Mettupalayam or Coimbatore. As vast area is under Eucalyptus plantation, manufacture of Eucalyptus oil is pursued as a cottage industry. The important factory in the public sector is the Hindustan Photo Films Manufacturing Company Limited. Other factories are the Cordite Factory, Food Specialities Limited, Protein Products of India Limited, Needle Industries (India) Private Ltd., and Ponds (India) Private Limited.

Trade and Commerce

The Chief articles of trade in the district are tea, coffee, vegetables, fruits, timber, eucalyptus oil, garlic and pepper. The products grown here are marketed both at Udhagamandalam and Mettupalayam.

The Coonoor ghat road which connects Mettupalayam and Coonoor forms the main communication line from plains to Udhagamandalam. The Siriyur ghat road starts from northern crest of the plateau and passes through Masinagudi and Theppakadu. At Gudalur, it joins the State Highway from Calicut passing through Cherambadi. As per the data available, the total length of roads is 1625 kms, out of which 1071 kms. are surfaced and 554 kms. are unsurfaced. A hill railway connects Ooty with Mettupalayam in the plains.

Ecological Importance

The significance of Nilgiris in ecological terms is immeasurable. Given the physiographic differentiation of the Nilgiris district, the area harbours a wide variety of bio-climates and vegetation that is unique in peninsular India.

In a short distance of 50 km the average annual rainfall ranges between 1000 mm and 3000 mm and the altitude varies between 300 M and 2600 M. This variation endows the area with a variety of vegetation types from evergreen forests to scrub jungles and provides a diversity of environments.

The extremely fragile ecosystem in Nilgiris sustains a wide variety of biological resources and supports human existence in the hills as well as the surrounding plains. The resources generated in terms of water, energy and other forest products have a significant impact on the region's economy. Sholas are referred to as "living fossil" by forest researchers because, if disturbed, they can never stage a return to the forest physiognomy. The initial micro climatic factors that prevail in the degraded areas never allow the tropical stock of sholas to regenerate[4].

Economic Significance

The Economic benefits derived from the resources of Nilgiris for the people in the district, the state and country are also immense. The major benefit areas are as follows:

Plantation and Horticulture

Nilgiris has a share of 26 per cent of the total green tea produced in India. The significance of tea in the Nilgiris is elaborated in a separate Chapter. Contribution of other plantation and horticultural crops is indicated in Table 3.4.

TABLE 3.4

HORTICULTURAL CROPS OTHER THAN TEA – 1992-93

Crops	*Total Area Ha*	*Quantity Kg*	*Value of production Rs. in Crores*
Coffee	7910	5932500	93.56
Cardamom	1102	101384	15.68
Fruits	1731	10484667	67.84
Pepper	2073	393870	20.88
Other Vegetables	3881	84937742	167.33
Total	19564	176640914	496.16

Source: Price Waterhouse, 1997, HADP Evaluation Report P.11.

Hydel Power/Irrigation

The district is drained by a number of streams. All of them eventually drain either into the Moyar flowing eastwards, north of the district or into the Bhavani flowing to the South of the district. The capacity, production and value of energy produced by the hydel power stations in Nilgiris may be seen in Table 3.5.

The Nilgiris hydel power capacity constitutes about 34 per cent of Tamil Nadu's total Hydel Power Capacity. In terms of overall energy produced including thermal stations, the Nilgiris share is around 12 per cent.

Hundreds of hectares of lands in three surrounding States are also getting irrigated through rivers originating from Nilgiris. The Bhavanisagar dam is estimated to provide irrigation to 2.4 lakhs acres in the dry areas of Coimbatore and Erode districts. Water from the Bhavani river is also pumped to Coimbatore and Tiruppur towns – major centres for industrial and export activities.

TABLE 3.5
INSTALLED CAPACITY AND GENERATION: STATION-WISE

Power House	*Installed Capacity (MW) as on 31.3.92*	*Generation (MU) 1993-94*	*Value of Energy Produced*
Hydro Station			
1. Pykara	70	348	452.40
2. Moyar	36	142	184.60
3. Kundah-I	60	282	366.60
4. Kundah-II	175	709	921.70
5. Kundah-III	180	407	529.10
6. Kundah-IV	100	147	191.10
7. Kundah-V	40	64	83.20
8. Pykara Micro	2	10	13.00
9. Lower Bhavani	4	37	48.10
Total Nilgiris	667	2146	2789.80
Other Districts	1276.25	2427	3155.10
Total Hydel Power	1947.75	4573	5944.90
Total Power	4314.75	16364	21273.20

Source: Price Waterhouse 1997, HADP Evaluation Report, P.11.

Developmental Issues in Nilgiris

The population of Nilgiris has increased from a mere 3000 in 1812 to around seven lakhs in 1991. A very large part of this high growth rate of population is due to immigration of people from the backward districts of the surrounding States. The power projects in early fifties, the immigrants rehabilitation policy of 1960's and growth in plantation sector subsequently aided this growth.

The cumulative average growth rate of population in Nilgiris since 1941 to 1991 is around 2.5 per cent as against the growth rate of 1.5 per cent for the entire State of Tamil Nadu. If total area is considered, the density of population of the Nilgiris (277 per sq. km) is less than that of the State (429). However, this is deceptive. A better picture will emerge if forest area is excluded. In that case, the density in the Nilgiris becomes 632 against a comparable figure of 519 for the State. The high density of population in Nilgiris is an indicator of the pressures on the carrying capacity of Nilgiris .

As indicated earlier, the population growth in Nilgiris is mainly by migration of human groups into the area rather than a natural growth of indigenous groups. Nilgiris is one among the 7 districts which have net positive migration in Tamil Nadu.

Plantation workers constitute the largest proportion of the migrants. The dependent female migrants along with the labour also seem to be very high as reflected in the non worker migrants proportion. Migrants to Nilgiris originate from drought-prone, economically underdeveloped southern districts of Tamil Nadu or under developed districts of Kerala. A significant proportion of migrants is from the economically weaker section of the society. The proportion of schedule caste in Nilgiris (30.2 per cent) is higher than the State average 19.2 per cent.

Land Use and Ecological Implications

The human intervention in Nilgiris has significantly altered the land-use pattern in Nilgiris. The major changes in this region can be summarized as follows:

- Planting of exotics for industrial purpose in grass lands as well as in sholas till recently. (The Forest Department, Government of Tamil Nadu has taken a policy decision recently to stop further growth of pulpwood area).

- Tea and other plantation crops replacing natural forests.

TABLE 3.6
LAND-USE PATTERN IN NILGIRIS, 1905 TO 1992 (IN ACRES)

Year	*Area under Forest*	*Net Area under Cultivation*	*Current Fallows*	*Gross cropped Area*	*Area not available for Cultivation*	*Cropping Efficiency*
1905-1906	319,618	65,642	128,118	68,411	42,269	104.22%
1911-1912	344,099	69,024	124,894	72,055	48,570	104.39%
1921-1923	316,405	75,335	119,237	79,532	49,529	105.57%
1931-1932	311,052	84,225	147,628	89,586	46,710	106.37%
1941-1942	309,622	99,301	132,301	106,080	40,489	106.83%
1951-1952	342,156	102,758	35,153	108,293	30,921	105.38%
1957-1958	341,952	113,571	18,530	116,079	41,181	102.21%
1958-1959	341,952	116,230	17,494	120,568	41,208	103.73%
1959-1960	341,952	117,544	15,790	122,236	41,208	103.99%
1960-1961	341,686	120,111	13,741	125,126	41,175	104.18%
1970-1971	342,793	134,074	10,242	134,775	38,553	100.52%
1980-1981	352,138	144,580	29,281	147,417	33,778	101.96%
1991-1992	353,971	173,714	28,847	174,528	28,306	100.47%

Source: Price Waterhouse, 1997, 'HADP Final Evaluation'. P.20

TABLE - 3.7

LAND-USE PATTERN – TALUK-WISE – 1991

Hectares

Classification	*Ooty*	*Coonoor*	*Kothagiri*	*Gudalur*	*Nilgiris*
Total area	119764	22769	39666	72172	254381
Forest	80633	4889	20204	37633	143359
Barren and Uncultivable	1668	3	691	350	2712
Non-Agricultural use	3138	2268	1354	1992	8752
Cultivable waste	1286	8	1213	368	2875
Permanent Pastures and Grazing Land	1838	478	2040	362	4718
Land under Misc. Tree Crops, etc.	1674	2	212	318	2206
Current Fallows	6945	1081		3657	11683
Other Fallows	3770	208	2044	1700	7722
Net area sown	18812	13842	11908	25792	70354

Source: Price Waterhouse, 1997, HADP Evaluation Report.

- Promotion of Annual crops especially potato.
- Conversion of annual crop lands to horticulture plantations especially tea.
- Encroachment and land grabbing in the Gudalur Jenmam lands.

Table 3.6 shows the land use pattern in Nilgiris since the beginning of this century based on various land based records/assessment

The land based records are very broad indicators of the ground realities. The data reflects more of the ownership pattern rather than actual coverage. Still, the significant increase in the total cropped area is of critical concern from ecological point of view. Table 3.7 provides taluk wise land use pattern in Nilgiris.

It can be observed that Forest areas of Nilgiris are primarily concentrated in the Ooty and Gudalur taluks. 60 percent of the area in Coonoor taluk is under cultivation.

Cropping Pattern

While the overall ratio between forest area and cultivated area is of critical importance, the changes within the cultivated area also assume importance in the context of the very high level of soil erosion. Table 3.8 provides the cropping pattern changes in the last four decades.

TABLE - 3.8
CROPPING PATTERN IN NILGIRIS

	Area of cultivation (In Hectares)			
	1960-1961	*1970-1971*	*1980-1981*	*1992-1993*
Tea	17897	22711	26997	46619
Coffee	8957	8690	8964	7910
Banana	614	512	197	292
Citrus Variety	336	206	237	1012

Contd.'

	Area of cultivation (In Hectares)			
	1960-1961	*1970-1971*	*1980-1981*	*1992-1993*
Other Fruits	95	206	124	427
Cardamom	98	185	305	1102
Pepper	71	106	357	2073
Ginger	205	573	380	887
Potatoes	9486	8131	7023	2867
Other Vegetables	922	1820	3926	3881
Others	9964	11160	10040	3284
Gross Cultivated	48645	54300	58550	70354

Source: Price Waterhouse, 1997, HADP Evaluation Report, P.22.

CHANGING CROPPING PATTERN

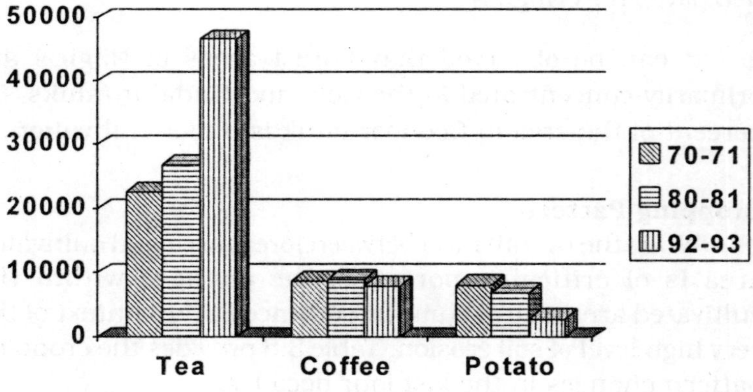

There has been a significant shift from annual crop cultivation to perennial crop cultivation and especially tea cultivation. The share of area under perennial crop has increased to 62 per cent in 1993 from 37 per cent in 1960. During the same period the annual crop share has decreased to 10 per cent from 22 per cent.

Environmental Problems of the Nilgiris

The degradation of the environment, ecology and natural beauty of Nilgiris is too well established and documented to give room for any doubt. The Geological Survey of India, after a detailed study concluded "the stage of preventing environmental degradation in Nilgiris has been crossed over. The harm has been done. The present stage is one of repairing the damages. It is fundamental that the cost of repair or cure is always more than the cost of prevention". Environmental problems in the Nilgiris can be broadly discussed under three headings. (1) Land use changes, (2) Extension of Monoculture and (3) Urbanisation.

Land Use Change and its Consequences

Settlers in Nilgiris induced numerous changes in the land cover. Natural forests and grasslands gave way to extensive cultivation of tea, coffee, cinchona, bluegum, wattle, peaches, pears, plums, oranges, potato, temperature vegetables, etc.

Out of these induced changes, maximum change and havoc was created by tea, coffee, potato and vegetable crops without adoption of suitable conservation measures resulting in heavy soil loss and runoff besides spoiling the mountain landscape and beauty of the region.

In the recent years, the destruction of native "Shola" forests and grasslands and the cultivation of tea by clearing new areas on steep slopes has resulted in the drying up of some of the tanks and streams. The local balance of nature has been badly upset during the last three decades and an anxious era of land slides and flash floods on one hand and droughts on the other has started in the Nilgiris causing considerable havoc. Conversion of forest lands into agricultural lands under "Grow more food campaign", encroachment on more and more forest lands and grasslands to meet the food, fuel and fodder requirements of the unchecked human and animal population with utter disregard to the soil, topography and climatic conditions, adoption of exploitative methods of cultivation, etc., have been the main causes of severe soil erosion and its attendant evils .

Studies conducted at the Central Soil and Water Conservation Research and Training Institute, Research Centre, Udhagamandalam indicated high amounts of soil loss in potato cultivation on slopes. Ill managed newly established tea plantation without soil and water conservation measures also contributed to heavy soil loss.

The sedimentation studies conducted by the Institute of Hydraulics and Hydrology, Poondi under the Watershed Management Board of the Tamil Nadu Government indicate 31.56 and 38.90 per cent loss in storage capacity due to siltation in Pegumbahalla and Pillur reservoirs respectively over a period of 16 years between 1966 and 1982 and 57.8 per cent in Kundahpallam reservoir over a period of 22 years between 1960 and 1982 while the Emerald Avalanche Reservoir has lost only 7.05 per cent of its capacity over a 20 years period between 1961 and 1981. All the three reservoirs are located in the Kundah system of reservoirs in the Bhavani River Basin.

The low rate of siltation in the Emerald-Avalanche Reservoir is due to the coverage of over 90 per cent of the catchment area under forests and tea estates. The same is the case of Pykara reservoir with well managed forest catchments which has not silted much since its construction in 1932.

The faulty land use adversely affects the hydrological cycle by inducing increased runoff and reducing recharge resulting in decreased length of flows in perennial streams and consequently water scarcity during the lean flow periods. It also affects the water quality due to washing down of chemicals such as fertilizers and pesticides affecting the quality of life. These various factors result in environmental degradation .

Extension of Monoculture

The results of hydrological studies conducted on two identical catchments at the Glenmorgan Farm of the

Research Centre (CSWCRTI) on conversion of natural grasslands into manmade forests of Eucalyptus globulus (bluegum) from 1968 onwards have indicated significant reduction in stream flow during this period due to conversion. Similar trends were also observed in the case of the other fast growing species viz., Acacia mearnsil (black wattle) in Parson's valley catchment. As such, caution has been recommended while planning large scale conversion of grasslands into plantations of fast growing species particularly Eucalyptus in the catchments of the Nilgiri reservoirs.

Of late, tea is receiving attention from a commercial point of view through Government subsidies. Though the canopy of tea bushes when fully developed can prevent erosion to a considerable extent, there is tremendous soil loss till the canopy is developed. Most of the tea plantations, owned by small farmers do not have tea canopy closed even after ten years due to bad management and inadequate inputs. Besides, the bench terraces used for raising of annual crops like potato are dismantled haphazardly by bringing them back to the original slope to accommodate more number of tea plants which results in accelerated erosion with its attendant evils[5].

Urbanisation

Urban development in Nilgiris is in chaos. Ooty, at one time the Queen of Hill stations, is now not much different from any market town in the surrounding plains. The Coonoor town "seems to have grown of its own accord without any control over the years". Gudalur and Kothagiri are fast going the way of Ooty and Coonoor, overburdened by the influx of repatriates and encroachers. Civic amenities have become woefully inadequate. Drinking water has become perennially scarce. Sewerage system has broken down and roads have become intolerable. During summer season the situation becomes worse as lakhs of tourists arrive.

The most disturbing aspect is the high level of speculation in real estate which has sent rentals and land prices to incredible heights. No slope is too steep for construction, notwithstanding the warning of GSI to avoid the slopes. Again, against the advice of GSI, most of the structures are multi-storied and heavy. In short, the urban setting can be described as ugly and unsafe.

The urban decay in the Nilgiris is largely the result of over population, excessive commercialization and near absence of town planning. The surge in recent years in investments in Nilgiris by outsiders is another contributing factor. Less than 3 per cent of the area is available for non-agricultural use in Nilgiris against an average of about 13 per cent for the entire State. This is all the more reason that the limited area available has to be properly planned so as to meet the various urban requirements and to retain the popular charm[6].

Summary

This Chapter has attempted to profile the district and mention the special significance of the district. The major issues in development of the district as seen from plans of HADP and the evaluation report of a professional body are listed. The concerns expressed by an environmental group are mentioned.

References

1. Government of Tamil Nadu (1995) – Gazetter of India, Tamil Nadu State, The Nilgiris District, Ed: M.Gopalakrishnan.

2. SAMMCRC (1990), *Project Kurinji – Nilgiris Integrated Energy Perspective*, Shri AMM Murugappa Chettiar Research Centre, Chennai-113.

3. HADP Cell, 'Hill Area Development Programme (1997), The Nilgiris, An Approach Paper', Ootacamund.

4. Price Waterhouse (1997), *'HADP Evaluation-Final report'*, Price Waterhouse, 610 Anna Salai, Chennai-6, pp. 8-22.

5. Government of Tamil Nadu (1994), Statistical Handbook of Tamil Nadu, Department of Statistics, Anna Salai, Chennai-6, pp. 29-49.

6. Save Nilgiris (1990), *Intensive Environmental Education*, Pamphlet by Save Nilgiris Campaign, Ootacamund, pp. 4-9.

4

Hill Area Development Programme The Macro View

The Union Planning Commission recognised the frailty of the eco-systems in Hill Areas and came up with Programmes of special Central Assistance (SCA) for Development of Hill Areas from the Fifth plan period. Two programmes called Hill Area Development Programme (HADP) and Western Ghats Development Programme (WGDP), were launched during the Fifth Plan. Both are in operation since then.

Coverage

The major Hill Areas of the country can be grouped as follows:

1. Areas which are co-extensive with boundaries of the State or Union Territories, namely Jammu and Kashmir, Himachal Pradesh, Sikkim, Manipur, Meghalaya, Nagaland, Tripura, Arunachal Pradesh and Mizoram.

2. Areas which form part of a State, which are termed as 'Designated Hill Areas', namely:

(a) Two hill districts of Assam – North Cachar and Karbi Anglong.

(b) Eight districts of Uttar Pradesh – Dehradun, Pauri Garhwal, Tehri Garhwal, Chamoli, Uttar Kashi, Nainital, Almora, Pithoragarh.

(c) Major part of Darjeeling District of West Bengal.

(d) *Nilgiris District of Tamil Nadu*

(e) 163 talukas of Western Ghats area comprising parts of Maharashtra (62 talukas), Karnataka (40 talukas), Tamil Nadu (29 talukas), Kerala (29 talukas) and Goa (3 talukas).

The Hill States mentioned at (1) above are called 'Special Category States'. The amount required for giving Central Assistance for their development plans is pre-empted from the divisible pool before making allocations from it to the other States categorized as 'Non-Special Category States'.

The hill areas covered under the programme of Special Central Assistance (SCA) are the areas identified in 1965 by a Committee of the National Development Council (NDC) and those recommended in 1972 by the High Level Committee for Western Ghats. 163 Talukas in the Western Ghats referred to above are covered by the Western Ghats Development Programme. The other 'Designated Hill Areas' mentioned above are covered by the Hill Area Development Programme. Nilgiris District of Tamil Nadu is one of the designed Hill Areas covered by HADP.

Scale and Pattern of Funding

Special Central Assistance is given by the Planning Commission to State Governments to meet the full expenditure under HADP. The total fund available is first divided[1] between designated districts for HADP and designated taluks for WGDP in the ratio 86.69:13.31. The amount available for the district is distributed among them with equal weightage to area and population[2]. This is the amount allocated under HADP. The other amount available for 163 taluks is distributed among them with 75 per cent weightage for area and 25 per cent weightage for population. This is the allocation under the Western Ghats Development Programme.

Outlays available for HADP in the Seventh and Eighth Plans are shown in Table 4.1.

TABLE – 4.1
OUTLAY FOR HILL AREAS

Rs. in Crores

	Seventh Plan Outlay	*Seventh Plan* Actual Allocation	*Eighth Plan* Outlay
A. Designated Hill Districts Total	753.50	924.03	1235.62
Assam	118.20	114.34	194.34
Tamil Nadu	33.75	41.53	55.49
Uttar Pradesh	553.50	679.19	910.04
West Bengal	44.55	55.04	73.25
Surveys & Studies	3.50	3.93	2.50
B. Designated Taluks of Western Ghats Regions	116.50	143.77	191.03
Total (A)+(B)	870.00	1067.80	1426.65

Objectives of HADP

The Hill Area Development Programme was initiated in the Fifth Five Year Plan. However, the Plan document for the 5th plan prepared by the Government of India, Planning Commission does not deal with the programme specifically.

The Sixth Plan document[3] has devoted a Chapter to Hill Area Development. Chapter 25 begins with the following:

It is now recognized that the pathways of development adopted in the past have resulted in an uneven distribution of the benefits of economic growth as between geographical areas and also between socio-economic groups. It was in realization of this phenomenon that certain specific target group oriented programmes, such as SFDA and MFAL were initiated during the Fourth and Fifth Five Year Plan periods.

Special Programmes for drought-prone, desert and tribal areas were also initiated. But in spite of these programmes, certain geographical areas present some very special ecological and socio-cultural features, which unless specifically taken into account, do not permit the present planning process and the schemes developed within it, to be of major assistance to them. The Hill Areas of the country belong to this category. The development of the hilly areas in the country, however, cannot be undertaken in isolation from the adjoining plains, with which their economy is closely inter-related. The hilly areas influence to some extent the climate of the plains; they contain the sources, the catchments and the water-sheds of several major river systems which flow to the plains. They abound in forests, plant and mineral wealth as well as hydel energy resources. Our experience of development planning during the last three decades has increasingly underlined the fact that unless adequate programmes are evolved for the conservation and proper utilization of the resources of the hill areas, not only the problems of these areas will continue to remain unsolved, but the economy of the plains may also be adversely affected. Symptomatic of this aspect are the rapid siltation of dams, reservoirs, flooding, changes in agro-climatic conditions and pressure on the employment market because of the large scale migration of people particularly men from hill areas. Development of the resources of the hill areas is hence necessary in order to enable the population living in these areas, who are by and large very poor, to have their share of the benefits accruing from modern science and technology. But such development, however, has to proceed in a way that the eco-system constituting the hills and the plains is not irreversibly damaged, but is preserved in a suitable condition for future generations. There is, therefore, a paramount need for conceiving an integrated strategy for the development of the hill areas based on sound principles of ecology and economics. It was in realization of this need that special hill area development programmes were initiated during the Fifth Plan. During the Sixth Plan also, the hill areas of the country will continue to receive special attention on account of their difficult terrain, agro-climatic conditions, historical lag in economic development, their environmental impact on the plains and above all, their great growth potential.

The documents deals with the need for conservation of the environment and states:

The hill area, particularly, the Himalayan region is rich in genetic material of medicinal and food plants, fruits, including citrus and a wide range of other economic plants, orchids and other flowers. Some rare wild life still occurs in these areas. It would be important to have an integrated strategy for the preservation of the valuable flora and fauna through a chain of biosphere reserves, national parks and gene-sanctuaries.

The Seventh Plan document dealt with Hill Area Development in Chapter 16, as one of the Special Area Development Programmes and commented as follows:

The hill areas of the country, particularly the Himalayan and the Western Ghats regions which constitute about 21 percent of the total area and contain 9 per cent of the total population of the country, support the basic life giving natural resources but have fragile and sensitive eco-systems. The need to conserve natural resources and the environment, particularly to prevent damage to fragile and irreplaceable eco-systems, has been voiced in national policies and programmes for quite some time. The Hill Area Development Programme (HADP), in operation since the inception of the Fifth Five Year Plan, has been a major step in this regard. Simultaneously, it has also aimed at the goal of balanced regional development. During the Seventh Plan, the programme is expected to enter a crucial phase, particularly with reference to complementarity of interests of the hill and plains. The programme was tilted in favour of beneficiary-oriented schemes during the Fifth Plan period. In the Sixth Plan period, eco-development was emphasized, but the general tenor of the plans did not differ significantly from the normal State Plans. In other words, they have been characterized by the sectoral approach without adequate reference to eco-restoration, eco-preservation and eco-development. In the Seventh Plan, the emphasis will be on evolving plans which harmonise the three parameters, i.e., socio-economic growth, development of infrastructure and promotion of ecology. This implies consideration of ecological aspects at the time of formulation of policies, programmes and schemes.

The Eighth Five Year Plan document[1] deals with HADP in Chapter 17 (Special Area Development Programmes). The document summarises the problems of Hill Areas as follows:

The crucial environmental problems of the hills are deforestation and soil erosion, both leading to the drying up of water sources, flash floods and decline in the yield of food and cash crops, fodder, fuel and other minor forest produce. Poverty in the hills is directly related to shortages of materials for basic subsistence, specially where, under the traditional land and water management systems, the capacity of land to support the population has already been exceeded.

The Eighth Plan[1] deals with the objectives, Approaches and Strategies of HADP in some detail as follows:-

The programme has been in operation since the inception of the Fifth Five Year Plan in the Designated Hill Areas. The basic objective of the Hill Areas Development Programme has been socio-economic development of the hills and the people living there in harmony with ecological development. The programmes implemented under the HADP have, therefore, aimed at promoting the basic life support systems with sustainable use of the natural resources of the area covered by the programme.

The approach and the strategy of the HADP has evolved over time. The programmes implemented during the Fifth Plan period were mainly beneficiary oriented. While the emphasis shifted to eco-development in the Sixth Plan, the general tenor of the HADP remained substantially the same as that of the normal State Plan following the same sectoral approach. The Seventh Plan laid particular emphasis on the development of ecology and environment as summed up in three phrases namely, eco-restoration, eco-preservation and eco-development. It aimed at evolving plans and programmes to take care of socio-economic growth, development of infrastructure and promotion of ecology of the areas covered by the HADP.

During the last three Five Year Plans, substantial efforts and resources were channelised for the development of infrastructure. However, the growth in the productive sectors of most of the hill economies has not kept pace with the extent of efforts and resources channelised. During the Eighth Plan, attention will have to be focused on this, especially, in modernizing the agricultural practices and small scale industries at household, cottage and village levels. To achieve this, involvement of the people, would be of paramount importance. Actual basic needs of the people have to be met through improved management of their land and water resources. The following will be the approach and strategy in respect of hill areas development planning.

Intensive efforts would be necessary at the implementation level to halt the process of degradation of the hills and improve productivity of land.

Innovative approaches to family planning and welfare to contain the population growth to sustainable levels have to be adopted. Financial and physical monitoring of the HADP by the State Governments would help improve implementation of various programmes.

Afforestation programme may be popularized through village Panchayat or village authorities, schools and other local organizations, groups and clubs. Private nurseries, especially, of multi-purpose trees which yield benefits like fodder leaves, edible fruits or leaves or flowers, seeds leaves of commercial value can be encouraged. Application of scientific inputs to agriculture and allied sectors, including identification of crops suitable for the agro-climatic zones, multi-purpose species of trees and bushes to meet requirements of the people from a well-developed small land area are of special importance. This approach is expected to spare considerable areas for permanent greening programmes, like social forestry or horticulture and serve the long-term objectives of enhancing production on sustainable basis. Appropriate technologies to bring about localized self-sufficiency and generate alternative means of livelihood, as opposed to heavy dependence on forests. Live-stock rearing, can be encouraged. Use of appropriate technologies to upgrade the traditional productive system like agricultural operations, livestock rearing, arts and crafts, household and cottage industries, etc., and to reduce drudgery of women in fetching water, fuel-wood, fodder and other demanding daily domestic chores needs to be encouraged on priority. The technologies have to be need-based, more productive, efficient, low-cost, and ecologically sustainable. Extension services should enlighten and educate people on how to enhance productivity of both cultivated and community land on a sustainable basis in the context of increasing human and livestock pressures. Consolidation of small and scattered land holdings would help in improving water and land management and ultimately, productivity of the limited land assets of the hills.

In many hill areas, land assets are held as common or community property. In such areas, people do not make permanent investments and several other problems also originate from this. To overcome these, local communities have to evolve suitable models of land management that would invite permanent investment and ensure both optimal returns and ecological safety and development. The State Governments may take a fresh look at their Plan and non-Plan Schemes, forest policies, land tenure systems, land and water use policies and realign them to eradicate practices destructive to ecology and environment.

In order to reduce pressure on land, quality of livestock, including goats, sheep, pigs and poultry birds has to be improved and their numbers reduced. There is an urgent need for relating livestock population to the bearing capacity of available land. Scrub animals could be systematically culled out. The livestock and cattle improvement programmes need to be integrated with fodder and cattle-feed development, stall feeding and scientific grazing. The land and livestock management systems have to improve rapidly. The productivity of pastures and grazing areas needs to be restored and enhanced. The effort should be to meet the requirements of food, fuel wood, timber and fodder through scientific utilization of scarce hill resources on sustainable basis from the least land area. Development of non-conventional energy and use of non-wood based sources of energy could be encouraged. Development of watersheds that can meet water requirement of the people and conserve water and soil resources of the area can be taken up for integrated development. For this, a multi-disciplinary approach is considered most appropriate for creating conditions conducive to development of natural and human resources. Food security has to be ensured on top most priority. Development of horticulture, sericulture and plantation, especially cash crops having low volume, light weight, high value and long shelf-life, could play an important role in generating employment opportunities, higher income and ecologically sound development in hilly areas.

Area specific marketing infrastructure, especially for perishable produce and its processing, storage and packaging may be set up where such surpluses are imminent or evident.

At the household level, kitchen gardens can be popularized to supplement and enrich the diet of hill people.

Wherever transport linkages have been established and local cultivation of food grains is not advantageous, strong Public Distribution System could be extended, provided other adequate income generating avenues exist.

To reduce the use of wood for packaging of horticultural produce, suitable non-wood based packaging materials such as plastics could be increasingly used on a viable basis. Incentives that would encourage formation of large viable hill villages might be built into the development effort so that the overhead input costs to reach amenities and services to them, could be reduced. Many hill areas seem to be especially suited to industries like electronics, watch-making, optical glasses, sericulture, etc., that require pollution-free atmosphere, cool climate and precision skills. A number of cottage industries like carpet weaving, handlooms, handicrafts and other village and household based small scale industries can be encouraged. Due to higher transportation costs in these areas, industries which reduce weight and volume, but add value and increase shelf-life to the locally and medium industries may not generally be considered suitable except under favourable circumstances. Rubber plantations have proved successful in certain areas. Wherever degraded tree-free land could become available and where rubber plantations could thrive, these could be encouraged. Development of sericulture has good potential in hill areas. A systematic programme of planting feedstock trees for silkworms on all spare patches of land can be taken up. Development of sericulture can provide employment to educated and skilled workers and generate value adding activities and bring in foreign exchange. However, the programme will call for right quality of grain, prompt payment in cash for the cocoons and primary processing activities at local levels.

Tourism can be organized as an industry, with due care taken to avoid exploitive use of scarce local resources, especially, water and fuel-wood. Location specific suitable code of conduct for tourists may be evolved so as to maintain the surroundings clean and disease free, protect local ecology and respect local traditions, culture and heritage. Special care needs to be taken to ensure that hill roads are constructed as per the traffic needs, scientific design and specifications suited to hill areas, so that the loose soil is contained, proper drainage system is developed and chances of land slides are minimized. In such hill areas where the population density is low and the villages are small and scattered over long distances, porter or pony tracks can be built and properly maintained. Road construction should be completed in all respects without delays. Mining can be carried out but with adequate safeguards in favour of ecology during and after the mining operations. Resources should not be thinly spread on a large number of projects and schemes. The priority for such ongoing and spill over schemes, projects and programmes which do not benefit people in improving their quality of life or are destructive to ecology, can be reduced down or terminated. Some of the voluntary organizations doing commendable work in the hills can be encouraged, especially, those engaged in improving the ecological system besides economic and social conditions of the people. People have to be made aware of the far reaching implications for environmental degradation and their active participation has to be sought for reconstruction of ecology. Environmental aspects can be suitably woven into the curriculum of primary and school classes. Regeneration and development of the hill environment cannot be achieved without willing and active cooperation of the people. It will be forthcoming, only if the benefits from improved land, water and forests resources, reach directly and equitably to the people themselves. The hill areas prone to intense tectonic and seismic activities, need to be identified. Activities like indiscriminate road and building construction and creation of artificial large water bodies, need to be minimized and earthquake-proof designs should be used in construction. Large projects etc., which might endanger the ecological balance and displace large number of people should be very carefully considered before investment decisions are taken. Families whose agricultural land is acquired should be settled with productive assets. In many hill areas, men folk have migrated to towns and plains in search of employment opportunities. In such areas, women are managing land and other economic assets. The approach and policies should keep this in view, especially for lightening their burdens of daily chores like collection of fuel-wood, water, and tending to livestock and other domesticated animals and birds. It will be of much advantage if women extension workers are appointed in such villages.

Summary

A study of the Five Year Plans indicates that the national objective of the HADP has evolved over the years into one of sustainable development of the Hill Areas. The HADP has aimed to achieve Eco-restoration, eco-protection and eco-development of Hill Areas in a sustainable manner. The Plans have noted that their objectives require multi-sectoral approach in the HADP. The Plans have set out various types of scheme which can be considered. The list of recommended schemes is long. Considering these permissible schemes, specific programmes have been devised for each hill area, taking note of the local features, problems and requirements. For the Nilgiris district, Five Year and Annual Plans for HADP are drawn up by the State Government of Tamil Nadu. After consideration, modification and approval by the Union Planning Commission, the HADP is implemented by the Government of Tamil Nadu as a Centrally Assisted Scheme.

References

1. Government of India (1992), Planning Commission, *Eighth Five Year Plan 1992-97*, Vol.II, pp. 426-438.
2. Government of India (1985), Planning Commission, *Seventh Five Year Plan 1985-90*, Vol.II, pp. 338-343.
3. Government of India (1980), Planning Commission, *Sixth Five Year Plan (1980-85)*, pp. 413-416.

5

HADP in the Nilgiris— A Micro Analysis

The Hill Area Development Programme in the Nilgiris District is being implemented by the Government of Tamil Nadu, since inception of the Fifth Five Year Plan. The State Government has adopted eco-restoration, eco-preservation and eco-development, while taking care of the socio-economic and developmental needs of the district, as the basic objectives of Hill Area Development Programme in the Nilgiris.

From the Seventh Five Year Plan, emphasis has been laid on schemes which harmonize three parameters, namely socio-economic growth, development of infrastructure and conservation and preservation of ecology. There has been a gradual shift from "individual beneficiary oriented" approach to "area based" approach.

Formulation and Implementation

The Union Planning Commission (UPC) has issued guidelines for preparing the HADP. The UPC also issues modifications from time to time to the Planning and Development Department in the Secretariat. Planning and Development is in charge of drafting, implementing and monitoring the Hill Area Development Programme at the State level. At the district level, the Collector coordinates the formulation of the HADP and monitors its implementation. About six months prior to commencement of the next financial year, Planning and Development Department calls for proposals for the next year from heads of various departments implementing the HADP and from the Collector of the Nilgiris district. The departments are also advised to keep in view the guidelines of the UPC and consult the Collector before sending their proposals. After considering the proposals, Planning and Development Department drafts its plan proposals. Keeping in view the guidelines, the priorities and the likely availability of funds, the draft Plan is critically examined by the UPC and approved with necessary modifications. After the Budget for the relevant financial year is passed by Parliament, the UPC communicates the allocation of funds, sector-wise to the State Government. Thereafter, Planning and Development Department issues orders allocating funds scheme-wise under each sector. Schemes are implemented and expenditure incurred by departmental officers in the district with reference to the orders of Planning and Development Department and in accordance with their respective departmental codes.

For implementing the programme, special staff has been sanctioned in Forest, Agricultural Engineering, Horticulture, Geology, Evaluation and Public Works Departments. For Planning and monitoring work, special staff has been sanctioned in the Secretariat and in Nilgiris district. A Project Director working under the Collector, heads the HADP Cell in the Nilgiris District.

It may be noted that the HADP is implemented as a collection of sectoral programmes implemented by the Heads of Department. While the Collector monitors the programme, the responsibility for formulation and implementation rests mainly with the Heads of the Department.

Total Outlay

The outlay on HADP in Nilgiris District has grown from Rs. 9.97 crores in the Fifth Plan to Rs. 85.95 crores in the Eighth Plan. These figures are in terms of nominal values for different periods. For better appreciation, it would be desirable to compare the investment in real terms, after providing for inflation during this period. For this purpose, the index for the mid-year of each plan may be considered and the outlays compared after reducing them to the price-level of 1976, the mid-year of the Fifth Plan. Outlays in nominal terms and in terms of 1976 prices, are listed in Table 5.1.

TABLE - 5.1
TOTAL OUTLAY IN NOMINAL AND REAL TERMS

(Rs. in Lakhs)

Plan & years	*Outlay*	*Mid-Year*	*Index No. for Mid-Year **	*Outlay in 1996 prices*	*Percentage Increase*
Fifth 1974-1979	997.00	1976	172.4	997.00	—
Sixth 1980-1985	2383.00	1982	285.3	1448.00	44
Seventh 1985-90	4062.78	1987	395.7	1770.09	23
Eighth 1992-97	8595.00	1994	753.3	1967.05	11

* Whole-sales Price Index 1971=100

Source: Tata Services Ltd., Department of Economics and Statistics, Statistical Outline of India, 1995-96. p-197.

The last column in Table 5.1 shows the increase in outlay in successive Five Year Plans in terms of 1976 prices. The increase from 5th to 6th Plan was 44 per cent. This came down to 23 per cent and 11 per cent in the next two Plans. It discloses that in real terms also the Outlay has increased in successive plans; but the rate of step-up has declined. Increase from 5th to 6th Plan was 44 per cent. But the increases from 6th to 7th to 8th Plans were only 23 per cent and 11 per cent. It should be remembered that the figures relate to 5 year periods. The annual increase during the 8th Plan years was about 2.2 per cent only.

Sectoral Outlays

Forestry, horticulture, agriculture and soil conservation play a major role in ecological restoration. As such, maximum outlays have been provided to these three sectors. While ecological preservation and conservation has been the central theme of Hill Area Development Programme, the socio-economic development needs of the district have not been ignored.

The programme has been designed in such a way as to cater to these needs. Having these objectives in mind, other sectors such as health, medical, SC/ST, Human resources development, have been given substantial importance and funding[1].

For achieving the objectives of HADP, a multi-sectoral approach is being followed. During the 8th Plan, HADP covered as many as 27 sectors. All the 27 sectors and their relative shares are shown in Table 5.2.

Even though HADP covers many sectors, the investment is highly concentrated in Soil Conservation (22 per cent), Forestry (18 per cent) and Horticultural (14 per cent) sectors as may be seen from Table 5.2.

TABLE – 5.2
SANCTIONED OUTLAY IN VIII PLAN

Rs. lakhs (rounded)

Sl. No.	*Sector*	*Outlay*	*Percentage of Total*
1	Soil Conservation	1897	22
2	Forestry	1512	18
3	Horticulture	1220	14
4	Pollution Control of Ooty Lake	903	11
5	Roads	568	7
6	Welfare of SC/ST	284	3
7	Water Supply	253	3
8	De-silting of Ooty Lake	212	2
9	Human Resources Dev.	192	2
10	HADP Cell	187	2

Contd.

Sl. No.	Sector	Outlay	Percentage of Total
11	INDCO Tea Factories	170	2
12	Dairy & Animal Husbandry	147	2
13	Minor Irrigation	134	2
14	Tourism	133	2
15	Medical & Health	118	1
16	Remote Sensing	127	1
17	Eco-Sanitation	103	1
18	Khadi & Village Industries	85	0.9
19	Energy Conservation	74	0.9
20	Sericulture	68	0.8
21	Public Works Department	63	0.7
22	Eco-Development	40	0.5
23	Geo-Technical Cell	39	0.5
24	Technical Cell Secretariat	28	0.3
25	Evaluation	15	0.2
26	Fisheries	15	0.2
27	Nutrition	8	0.1
	Total	8595	100

Source: HADP Cell, Ootacamund

SECTORAL ALLOCATION

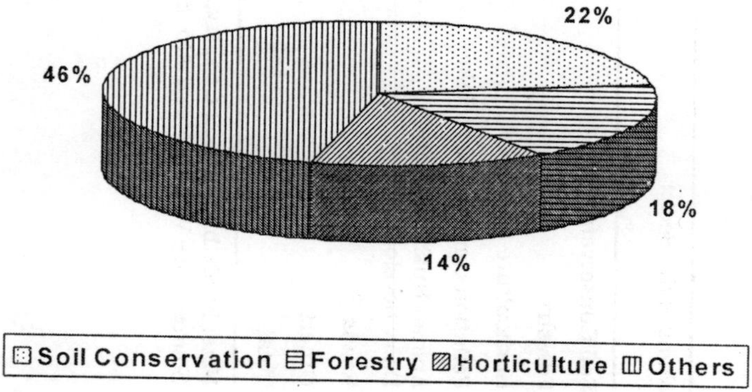

TABLE – 5.3
SECTORAL OUTLAY COMPARISION

(Rs. lakhs)

Name of the Sector	*Fifth Plan*		*Sixth Plan*		*Seventh Plan*		*Eighth Plan*	
	Outlay	% share	Outlay	% share	Outlay	% share	Outlay	% share
Soil Conservation	327.00	32.80	865.00	36.30	725.78	17.86	1896.67	22.06
Forestry	64.00	6.42	172.00	7.22	697.14	17.16	1515.60	17.63
Horticulture					1044.62	25.71	1220.33	14.19
Pollution control of Ooty lake							903.00	10.50
Animal Husbandry and Dairy development	219.00	21.97	238.00	9.99	217.37	5.35	147.54	1.72
Roads	187.00	18.76	646.00	27.11	560.00	13.78	567.66	6.60
Others	200.00	20.06	462.00	19.39	817.89	20.13	2347.20	27.31
Total	997.00	100	2383.00	100	4062.78	100	8595.00	100

Note: In Sixth Plan, Soil Conservation and Horticulture are put together.
Source: Price Waterhouse 1995, Evaluation of HADP, p-28.

The three sectors account for about 54 per cent of investment in the Eighth Plan. The other 24 sectors account for only 46 per cent. Reliance on these three sectors has been a feature of earlier Plans also. Allocations made for these major sectors during four plans are shown in Table 5.3.

It may be seen from the Table 5.3 that expenditure on Soil Conservation has varied from 32.8 per cent to 22 per cent. Forestry share has increased from 6.42 per cent to 17.63 per cent. Share of Horticulture has decreased between 25.71 per cent and 14.19 per cent. Dairy development had a significant share of about 22 per cent in the Fifth Plan which relied on beneficiary-oriented programmes. Its share has fallen thereafter to 1.72 per cent reflecting the change in emphasis. The case of the Roads sector brings out a dilemma in sustainable development of hill areas. Development of roads is essential for economic development of a region and improvement of higher educational and health facilities. Unfortunately, road development in and around forests leads to increased felling of trees and poaching of wild animals. Thus preservation of the forest environment suggests less investment on roads while general economic development needs higher investment on roads. The fluctuating share of roads between 27 per cent and 6.6 per cent reflects the effect of this dilemma.

Soil Conservation

In Nilgiris District, Soil erosion continues to be one of the most serious problems threatening the eco-system. It is well known that top soil loss is almost impossible to replace, resulting in poor agricultural yields and simultaneously silting up the down stream reservoirs in the plains. The most important causes of soil erosion are:

1. Denudation of permanent tree cover.
2. Inappropriate agricultural practices.

Under Hill Area Development Programme, the above two factors are sought tc be met by afforestation programme in the denuded slopes (under Forestry Sector) and conversion from annual crops to perennial crops in the agricultural lands (under Horticulture sector). Apart from these two major activities, Soil conservation measures per se are equally important to arrest soil erosion in the hilly terrain of the district.

The strategy adopted by the Agricultural Engineering Department has been to undertake various Soil Conservation measures as follows:

1. Treatment of Landslides.
2. Contour Stone walls.
3. Terrace Support walls
4. Staggered contour trenching
5. Afforestation
6. Revetments
7. Contour Stone walls with Staggered Trenching
8. Dry check and drop pits
9. Collection wells
10. Stream Training works
11. Construction of retaining wall to protect public buildings and roads which are affected due to heavy rains as remedial measures.

Soil erosion and landslips during rainy season have become regular features in Nilgiris District. The Geo-technical Cell established under HADP funding, after conducting detailed survey has recommended for taking various preventive measures to arrest landslides and soil erosion in coming years[1].

Forestry

Approximately 56 per cent of the total area in Nilgiris district comes under Forests as per the Revenue records. But aerial photographs and field surveys have indicated that the percentage of area occupied by natural and permanent tree cover is much less. Enlarging the permanent tree cover and regulating man's interference with nature, especially the forests, are the two prime objectives of the Hill Area Development Programme.

In order to maintain ecological balance as well as to restore the denuded areas priority has been given to Forestry Sector under Hill Area Development Programme. The strategy adopted by the Forest Department has been to undertake various measures as follows[1].

1. Re-clothing of denuded slopes and follow up cultural operation.
2. Soil and Moisture Conservation by constructing contour bunds.
3. Protection against encroachment by constructing cairns.
4. Protection of sholas and endangered plant species by chain link fencing.
5. Improvements to water sources for larger mammals.
6. Planting Rosewood and its associates.
7. Floristic restoration of semi-evergreen forests.
8. Deployment of Tribal watchers for anti-poaching activities.
9. Naturalization of exotic plantations.
10. Tree planting in urban areas.
11. Tribal Welfare schemes in R F areas.
12. Schemes to develop tourism in Wild life Sanctuary.

Pollution Control of Ooty Lake

Ooty lake is an important part of the environment of Ooty. The beautiful lake attracts many tourists. It also supports many types of aquatic fauna. The lake is getting polluted by sewage from the town. To control this pollution, a scheme to provide underground sewers, treat and pump the sewage away from the lake is being implemented.

Roads

Roads are most important life lines in Hilly Areas. Due to the hilly terrain, several villages still remain inaccessible due to the lack of road facilities. This severely hampers their economic progress. The hill economy cannot develop as a producing economy without an adequate and sufficient system of transport. At first sight, economic progress and preservation of ecological balance appear to be mutually exclusive. However the importance of the roads in an overall development strategy cannot be ignored.

As Dairy Development also plays a very vital role in the economy of the Nilgiris District, a good network of roads is essential to provide linkage to villages, to transport milk to chilling and processing center and agricultural produce for marketing. Under the Horticultural sector of the Hill Area Development Programme, more and more annual crop lands are being brought under perennial crops such as tea, fruit trees and silver oak trees. The small farmer who produces tea leaves has to necessarily send his produce to the tea factories which are at a considerable distance from the village. Therefore a good network of roads is essential for the marketing of tea which has come to be the mainstay in the economy of Nilgiris District. The strategy adopted by the Highways Department has been to improve the existing roads in the district on a priority basis[1].

Welfare of SC/ST

Scheduled castes and Scheduled Tribes constitute 23 per cent and 3.3 per cent respectively of the total population. Though the overall literacy of the District is 57 per cent, the literacy among the Scheduled Castes and Scheduled Tribes is very low. There are 23 Government Tribal Residential Schools for Scheduled Tribes students. These are in addition to regular schools run by Education Department. There are 15 hostels for Scheduled Caste Students. It is pertinent to point out that Nilgiris is not covered under Integrated Tribal Development Programme. Funds are being allotted by State Government for providing free education up-to higher secondary classes and also for free accommodation, free boarding, uniforms and text books free of cost. In addition to this, scholarships are also given. In order to supplement the efforts of State Government, the following schemes are taken under HADP[1].

1. Providing Dormitory buildings
2. Provision of basic amenities to Tribal Schools and Tribal colonies.
3. Other schemes for the uplift of Scheduled caste and Scheduled tribes in Nilgiris.

Rural Water Supply

Though the average annual rainfall in Nilgiris District is higher than in plains, protected drinking water has always been a scarce commodity in both Urban and Rural areas of this District. Provision of protected water supply to rural areas is an ongoing scheme, under Hill Area Development Programme.[1]

De-Silting of Ooty Lake

Ooty lake is over 150 years old. Considerable amount of siltation has taken place during these years. Consequently the lake has shrunk in area. To restore the area of water spread, HADP is supporting a scheme to desilt the lake.

Human Resource Development

To improve educational facilities in the district, additional buildings for schools have been constructed under the HADP.

INDCO Tea Factories

At present 17 Industrial Co-operative Tea Factories are functioning in Nilgiris District. They have enrolled a large number of growers owning small tea gardens. The Industrial Co-operative Tea Factories are providing continuous gainful employment to 1300 persons in the factories and 12000 farmers in the fields and indirect employment to 50,000 agricultural labourers. For modernizing the factories by replacement of old machinery and purchase of generators, financial assistance is provided under HADP to the Industrial Co-operative Tea Factories.

Animal Husbandry and Dairy Development

The Animal Husbandry Sector provides necessary back-up support for the Dairy Development activities in Nilgiris District. The total cattle population in Nilgiris District is roughly 1,30,000. Out of this, the breedable cattle population is roughly 70,000. In order to improve the breed of cattle for augmenting production of milk, financial assistance has been extended. The strategy adopted by the Animal Husbandry Department has been to take up the following measures to improve the cattle population/breed in the district.

1. Providing infrastructure to the veterinary health centers.
2. Animal Health Cover Programme
3. Animal Breeding Programme
4. Popularization of Frozen Semen technique.
5. Strengthening infrastructural facilities for augmentation of Fodder production in the fodder farms at District Livestock Farm and Kurthukuli Farm.
6. Tissue culture lab at Bokkapuram by NDCMPU Ltd., Udhagamandalam for faster multiplication of seed materials adaptable to the Nilgiris District.
7. Replacement of scrub animals in Masinagudi area.

Minor Irrigation

In the Nilgiris District there is no major irrigation source. The small farmers irrigate their crops by constructing check dams of mud across streams diverting the water. These mud dams have the inherent disadvantage of getting washed off during rainy season and cause flood damage to the fields. To mitigate the above problem, and to ensure regulated supplies to the fields, HADP has supported construction of small check dams of masonry with sluice arrangement.

Tourism

Nilgiris District has tremendous potential for tourism. Several places in this district like Udhagamandalam, Coonoor and the Mudumalai sanctuary are well known to tourists all over India and the world. The district is blessed with abundance of natural beauty and a variety of wild life. The salubrious climate is a major attraction to the tourists. In order to promote tourism while protecting the ecology of the district, financial assistance has been extended for eco-tourism.

Medical and Public Health

HADP has tried to improve medical assistance and public health to the public by creating basic infrastructural facilities through the following measures.

1. Construction of Out patient ward.
2. Construction of Residential Quarters.
3. Provision of Mobile Medical Units.
4. Provision of Ambulance.
5. Provision of Mortuary Vans.
6. Strengthening of Primary Health Centres and Staff quarters.
7. Providing Health sub-centres.
8. Purchase of essential equipment.

Remote Sensing

To help in preparation of water-shed based plans for developmental activities of different departments, appropriate maps have been prepared using Remote Sensing techniques. Based on interpretation of satellite imagery and aerial photographs, the maps have been prepared by the Institute of Remote Sensing, Anna University.

Other Factors

Small Outlays have also been provided for improving sanitation, promoting Village industries, sericulture and fisheries, encouraging energy conservation and for nutrition development. The mosaic of activities covered by HADP is very wide and some of the sectors are funded only marginally. However the main thrust has been on Soil Conservation, Forestry and Horticulture. Relative shares of all sectors may be seen in Table 5.2 already referred to.

Water Shed Plans

The Union Planning Commission considers that micro water sheds would form better units for planning the development of hill areas. It recommends formulation of an integrated development plan for each water-shed, involving activities of Forestry, Soil Conservation, Horticulture and other Departments. Typically the steep upper reaches would be amenable to forestry activities and the middle and lower reaches may be amenable to Horticulture and agriculture after appropriate soil conservation measures. A beginning has been made[5] in the Nilgiris District in preparing such water-shed plans for 1995-96.

The whole district has been delineated into watersheds[3] after an exhaustive study conducted by the Agricultural Engineering Department and the Institute of Remote Sensing of Anna University, Madras. The delineation is based on the guidelines followed in the Watershed Atlas of India, prepared by the Ministry of Agriculture, Government of India[6].

A watershed is basically that area which is covered by the tributary of a river or any drain passing through the area, starting from the ridge point to the drainage point. The Nilgiris district is drained by major rivers like Bhavani, Moyar & Kabini which are the tributaries of Cauvery and Pandiar respectively and Punnam Puzha, Karim Puzha and Chaliyar of Chaliyar basin.

The entire district has been delineated into 75 major watersheds on the basis of the above drainage pattern as shown in Table 5.4.

TABLE – 5.4
WATERSHEDS IN THE NILGIRIS

Sl. No.	*Reservoir*	*Sub Catchment*	*Watersheds*	*Total Number*
1	Lower Bhavani	Lower Bhavani	1 to 8	8
2	Lower Bhavani	Moyar	37 to 75	39
3	Pillur	Upper Bhavani	16 to 18	3
4	Kundah Geddai and Above Pillur	Kundah	9 to 15	7
5	Chaliyar	River Basin	19 to 36	18
		Total		75

Taluk-wise Details are as follows

Sl. No.	*Taluk*	*Watersheds*	*Total Number*
1	Ooty	11 to 19, 41 to 60, 64, 65 & 68	32
2	Coonoor	5 to 10	6
3	Kothagiri	1 to 4, 61 to 63, 66, 67, 69 to 75	16
4	Gudalur	20 to 40	21
		Total	75

Source: Department of Geology (1997), Geotechnical Cell, Coonoor

In the year 1984, the need to prioritize the watersheds was felt. Hence, the 75 watersheds were prioritized into 5 categories namely, very high, high, medium, low and very low according to the decreasing order of their silt yield index. The susceptibility and vulnerability to erosion, the frequency of landslides, human population, livestock population, land-use pattern etc., were the important factors based on which the status of the watersheds was decided. Environment and Bio-degradation were also reflected in the Silt Yield index based on which the watersheds were categorized.

Of the 75 watersheds, 28 very high and high priority watersheds were studied by Indian Space Research Organisation, Bangalore and by the Institute of Remote Sensing, Anna University, Madras. Based on their reports, 10 very high and high priority watersheds have been selected for the proposed plan as the others are covered by the Kundah River Valley Project. In addition, 5 minimum priority watersheds which are deteriorating very fast have also been selected.[7]

Table 5.5 indicates the degree to which the Plan was prepared on Watershed basis for 1996-97. Watershed plans accounted for 43 per cent of the total annual plan. Among the three main sectors, allocation to priority watersheds was 48 per cent of Soil Conservation. 61 per cent of Horticulture and 27 per cent Forestry.

TABLE – 5.5
EXTENT OF ADOPTION OF WATERSHED BASIS

Sector	*Amount proposed in selected watersheds*	*Other proposals*	*Total*
Soil Conservation	160.00	172.60	332.60
Horticulture	92.13	151.54	243.67
Forestry	73.06	267.65	340.71
Total	325.19	591.79	916.98
Other Sectors			1214.41
Grand Total			2131.39

Source: GOTN 1996, HADP Annual Plan Proposals 1996-97

Watershed planning is being tried seriously only from 1995-96. However, watershed plans cover only 43 per cent

1995-96. However, watershed plans cover only 43 per cent of the total. They are being prepared[8] just by putting together the programmes of three major departments in the selected watersheds. They are not strictly need based plans originating from the micro-level. There is also no involvement of local people in planning and implementation. HADP sectoral programmes are originating at the macro-level of Heads of Department. For the objectives of Watershed planning to be realized, it may be desirable to follow the principles of local area planning and let each Village Panchayat or a group of Panchayats identify the schemes needed for best development of the micro-watershed. After due refinement, these can be the water-shed plans. Involvement of local bodies in implementation is also desirable.

References

1. Government of Tamil Nadu (1992), Planning and Development, *HADP Eighth Plan Proposals, 1992-97.*

2. Government of Tamil Nadu (1995), Planning and Development Department, *HADP Annual Plan Proposals 1995-1996.*

3. Government of Tamil Nadu (1997), Department of Geology, Geo-technical Cell, Coonoor 'Note on land slides in Nilgiris'.

4. Government of Tamil Nadu (1994), Planning and Development Department, *HADP Annual Proposals, 1994-95.*

5. Government of Tamil Nadu (1995), Planning and Development Department, *HADP Annual Plan Proposals, 1995-96.*

6. Government of Tamil Nadu (1995(2)), Planning and Development Department, *HADP Annual Plan Proposals Integrated Watershed Development Plan 1995-96.*

7. Government of Tamil Nadu, (1996), Planning and Development Department, *HADP Annual Plan Proposals 1996-97.*

8. HADP Cell, Ootacamund, (1997), 'HADP – An approach paper'.

6

Development of Tea Cultivation in the Nilgiris

India is the largest producer of Tea in the world. It accounts for about 29 percent of the world production[1] Table 6.1 lists some of the important tea producing countries.

TABLE – 6.1
WORLD PRODUCTION OF TEA IN 1997

Country	*Production in Million Kgs.*
India	811
China	613
Sri Lanka	277
Kenya	221
Indonesia	154
Others	714
Total	2790

Source: Tea Board, Tea Statistics 1998. Page 72.

Within the country, Nilgiris District is a major tea producing district as may be seen from Table 6.2.

MAJOR TEA PRODUCERS

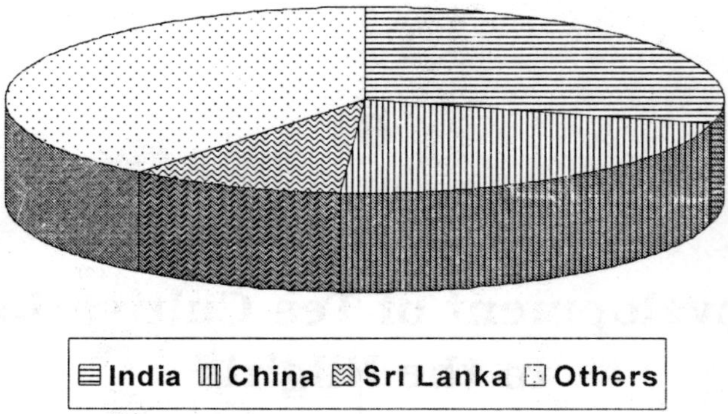

TABLE – 6.2
MAJOR TEA PRODUCING DISTRICTS IN 1997

Districts	*Area Under Tea (Hectares)*	*Production (thousand Kgs)*	*Productivity (kg/Hectare)*
Dibrugarh, Assam	71000	145668	2052
Dooars, W.Bengal	70539	132129	1873
Sibsagar, Assam	62751	109727	1749
Darrang, Assam	41700	81640	1958
Cachar, Assam	29534	49103	1663
Nilgiris, T.N.	35630	91672	2573
Idukki, Kerala	26745	52077	1947
All India	433759	810613	1869

Source: Tea Board Tea 1998, Page 6.

Among tea growing districts in the country, Nilgiris district has the fifth largest area under Tea. It stands fifth among these in annual production. It stands first in productivity.

Tea Cultivation and Production

The production of tea is influenced by several factors among which agro-climatic and economic factors are very important. Agro-climatic factors like climate, rainfall, soil type and economic infrastructural facilities like transport, communication, credit facilities, input supply and marketing affect the production of tea.

Being a perennial and location specific crop, tea comes up well in regions with an optimum altitude of 2000 feet to 5000 feet with the right soil type and climatic condition. Tea cultivation mainly depends upon the rainfall. For commercial cultivation of tea, it is essential that the soil should be acidic in nature, well drained and the area receives a minimum of 1250 mm of annual rainfall[2].

Tea seeds were planted in an experimental farm at Ketti in 1835. But the first field scale efforts to plant tea in the Nilgiris were on Thiashola and Dunsandle Estates in 1859.

Tea is a perennial crop with an economic life of 50-100 years. Many a South Indian Estate still has plants that were raised when the estate was first opened. Newly planted tea bushes require four years to attain maturity. They start yielding economic returns from the fifth year.

While a minimum of 40-50" of rainfall is considered sufficient to give an economic crop of tea, there are other variable factors relating to the season, such as prevailing air temperature, humidity and distribution of rainfall.

Tea cultivation is concentrated in the tracts where a heavy and well-distributed rainfall and a humid and equable climate permit of repeated flushings and plucking of the leaf. The soil must be rich and well drained and of a light nature. Elevations of 3,000 to 6,000 ft. are found suitable.

When the young plants have been in the ground for six months to a year they are cut down to about 6 to 8 inches from the ground. Each plant then throws out from the stump three to four shoots, and a bush is formed. After this, the bush is pruned back every two or three years. On it, the success of the crop largely depends, not only as regards quantity but also quality. The bushes as they flush that is, as the young shoots grow – are regularly plucked, and the young leaves and the tips of the young shoots taken off.

The plucking operation cannot be perfectly timed on a fixed schedule in an environment that cannot be standardized. But when the right time comes, plucking must be carried out so as not to risk long term damage to the bushes – even if the processing apparatus may not be ready for lack of power or some other reason. The leaf loses moisture and becomes rather flaccid within 24 hours. If not made into finished tea by then, the crop is a loss. This aspect has settled the question of factory location on or near the crop sites.

Plucked leaf is immediately brought into the factory and spread out in thin layers on trays of hessain, in shady sheds at the top of the factory, warmed by hot air. Here it 'withers' and becomes flaccid, and during the process, an enzyme is developed, which afterwards causes fermentation. When the withering is complete, the leaf, for orthodox manufacture, is put in a machine which rolls it to and fro on a table with a twisting motion. This presses out the juice on to the surface of the leaf. The rolled leaf is now allowed to ferment. It is placed for this purpose in layers, a few inches thick, in a moist, cool, darkened room. Fermentation finished, the leaf is dried, or 'fired' as quickly as possible in machines which drive a current of hot air over it.

After this, it is only necessary to grade it by means of sieves, and pack the tea in lead-lined, wooden cases for shipment to the markets.

While most of the advances in technology have brought about reduced consumption of energy and time at the factory, the C T C (Crush, Tear and Curl) method has resulted in a product that is of direct benefit to the consumer also. C T C tea makes upto 200 per cent more infusion than the crthodox variety and the increased cuppage explains its growing popularity in both home and export markets[3].

The climate is tropical and the fluctuation of temperature is minimum in the tea growing regions of the Nilgiris. The temperature ranges between 20 and 22.5 during South-West (June-September) monsoon and between 20 and 24 in the North-East monsoon season. Maximum temperature of about 27.6 is observed during hot weather (March-May) period (all temperatures in degree celsius).

A special feature of Nilgiris district is the large number of small estates as the figures in Table 6.3 show.

Small estates of 8.09 hectares (about 20 crores) or less account for 31 per cent of tea area and 97 per cent of tea-growers in the district. It is also significant to note that the total number of small estates in India is only 10,835 with an area of 97,369. Hence, small tea growers in Nilgiris represent 61 per cent of such growers in the country by number and 76 per cent of such growers by area.

TABLE - 6.3
SIZE-NUMBER AND AREA OF THE ESTATES IN NILGIRIS - 1996

Size in Hectares	*Number*	*Percentage of total number*	*Area in (hectares)*	*Percentage of Total Area*
Upto 8.09	25525	97.1	17103	31.3
8.09 to 50	135	1.9	2366	8.4
50 to 100	18	0.3	1248	4.7
100 to 200	21	0.3	3157	13.2
200 to 400	28	0.3	8219	26.4
Over 400	6	0.1	3492	16.1
Total	25733	100	35585	100

Source: Tea Board, Tea Statistics 1996-97, Page 24.25.

Area under Tea in Nilgiris district has increased in the last two decades. Table 6.4 shows the growth in area as per the Tea Board. Similar figures as per the Department of Statistics, Government of Tamil Nadu are shown in Table 6.5. There is a great divergence between the area figures from the two sources. It could be due to non-reporting of area by small farmers to Tea Board or other causes. However both sets of figures confirm increase in Tea Area.

The spectacular increase in tea area is due to the efforts of HADP as well as a number of other agencies in the Nilgiris District which are promoting tea cultivation. Some of the other agencies are UPASI, Tea Board, TANTEA and INCOSERVE. Their work is briefly mentioned below:

TABLE - 6.4
AREA UNDER TEA IN NILGIRIS DISTRICT AS PER TEA BOARD

Year	*Area in Hectares*
1961	20,840
1971	22,651
1981	24,849
1983	24,861
1989	25,827
1990	26,237
1991	26,260
1992	26,298
1993	26,423
1994	35,489
1995	35,537
1996	35,585
1997	35,630

Source: Tea Board. Tea Digest – 1999 – page 6

TABLE - 6.5
AREA UNDER TEA IN NILGIRIS DISTRICT

As per Department of Statistics, Government of Tamil Nadu:

Year	*Area in Hectares*
1980-81	26,997
1981-82	27,114
1982-83	26,362
1983-84	27,314
1984-85	28,709
1985-86	28,804
1986-87	38,454
1987-88	40,259
1988-89	40,847
1989-90	42,607
1990-91	45,043
1991-92	45,974
1992-93	46,619
1993-94	46,542
1995-96	47,903
1996-97	47,930

Sources: Department of Statistics, various Season Crops Report

GROWTH OF TEA AREA

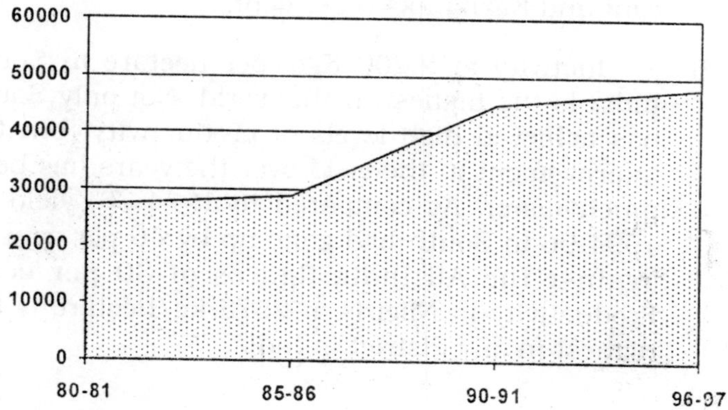

UPASI

The United Planters' Association of South India (UPASI), is a representative body of planters of Tea, coffee, natural rubber, cardamom and pepper in the States of Tamil Nadu, Kerala and Karnataka. In addition to being a forum to represent the cause of the planters, UPASI undertakes extension of R & D and advisory roles to help the planters. It also has schemes to help small and tribal farmers. UPASI has its headquarters in Coonoor. According to UPASI, some of the special features of tea plantations in South India[4] are:

1. The entire tea areas of South are located in hilly regions, in contrast to elsewhere in the country where tea estates are located in plains.

2. There is a large concentration of small growers, especially in Nilgiris district of Tamil Nadu and also in Idukki district of Kerala. Their number is estimated to be in the region of 40,000. The output of small grower sector is about 44 million Kgs., constituting 24 per cent of South India production.

3. To cater to the needs of small growers, there are over 100 'Bought Leaf Factories' and 17 Co-operative Factories in Nilgiris, who purchase the green leaf from the small growers for manufacture and sale.

4. State-wise, in South India, Tamil Nadu accounts for 62 per cent of the production. Kerala 35 per cent and Karnataka 3 per cent.

5. Productivity at 2,200 Kgs. per hectare in South India is the highest in the world. Not only South has achieved high levels of productivity, but the improvement in the yield over the years has been much faster. As compared to 1974-76, yield by 1994-96 in South had gone up by 46 per cent as against the All India figures of 30 per cent. Productivity in Nilgiris at 2573 kg/hectare is the highest in any district in India.

6. There has been sustained increase in production over the years. With the area available for expansion being limited, bulk of the production increase has come from yield improvement.

7. Between 1974-76 and 1994-96, tea output in South India increased from 106 million kgs. to 182 million kgs. (up by 72 per cent) Share of South India crop in All India production during this period went up from 21.3 percent to 23.8 percent.

8. There has been a significant shift towards manufacture of C.T.C. teas. While in 1974-76, the C.T.C./Orthodox ratio was 38.62, by 1994-96 it changed to 78.22.

9. Although there is a drastic decline in All India exports during the last four years, South has been maintaining its quantum of shipments. Consequently. share of South in All India exports has gone up from 20 per cent in 1974-76 to 40 per cent in 1994-96. Also, on an average, 34 per cent of South's production is shipped as against the All India figure of 20 per cent.

10. Practically, the entire instant tea exports from India emanate from South 1,700 tonnes valued at Rs. 40 crores were shipped in 1996.

11. Contrary to the virtual stagnancy in exports, domestic consumption of South India tea has been growing very fast. It doubled from 62 million Kgs. in 1974-76 to 120 million Kgs. in 1994-96.

Tea Board

The Tea Board has been set up by the Government of India to promote cultivation of tea, and production of made-tea for local consumption and export. The Tea Board administers many schemes to serve the above objectives. The Board has a regional office in Coonoor.

Out of the total tea production in Nilgiris, 64 per cent is contributed by the small growers sector. Therefore, this sector has great significance in South Indian tea industry. Tea Board has been attaching great importance to this segment of the industry and has been associated with its development for several decades. Tea growers having holding upto 10.12 ha are categorized as small tea grower for the purpose of availing assistance under the Tea Board small grower development schemes. Over the years Tea Board has formulated a number of schemes to assist small tea growers. They includes schemes for:

(a) Rejuvenation & consolidation of existing plantations.

(b) Replantation of bushes in old and uneconomic plantations.

(c) Crop Diversification scheme.

(d) Conversion of marginal lands held by Tribals into Tea.

(e) In-filling vacancies due to mortality of plants.

(f) Crop diversification through UPASI.

(g) Training of farmers through UPASI.

(h) Raising of tea-clones through INCOSERVE for distribution at subsidized rates.

Of these, the Crop Diversification Scheme has resulted in addition of significant area under Tea cultivation. Introduced in 1987 on pilot basis to enable small growers in Nilgiris to take up tea cultivation on a regular basis with assured small growers in Nilgiris to take up tea cultivation on a regular basis with assured income, this scheme has received enormous response from the small and marginal farmers. Out of the total 8845 ha vegetable land in Nilgiris, UPASI has identified 4000 ha suitable for tea cultivation. The scheme aims at encouraging conversion of this land to tea cultivation.

The scheme provides input subsidy at the rate of Rs. 15,000/- per ha out of which Rs. 12,500/- is payable as first instalment towards the cost of planting material Rs. 1,500/- as second instalment towards the cost of fertilizer, pesticides and Rs. 1,000/- as third instalment being the compensation for crop-loss. The scheme also provides payment of 5.1 per cent interest subsidy on a maximum amount of Rs. 16,000/- per ha of Bank loan for a period of four years following the year of planting[5]. While the assistance per capita is good, the total quantum of assistance is only about Rs. 35 lakhs[6] p.a. and is small in comparison with HADP expenditure on tea related schemes. But the extension work done by Tea Board, UPASI and Krishak Vigyan Kendra is valuable.

TANTEA

Another unique aspect of Nilgiris tea today is Government's participation in its growing. The Tamil Nadu Tea Plantation Corporation, popularly known as TANTEA, holds the unique distinction of having the largest area under clonal tea in India. It had its origins in 1968 as a Forest Department Project to provide employment to the people of Indian origin repatriated from Sri Lanka under the Sastri-Sirimavo Pact (1964). This project was converted into TANTEA in 1976. TANTEA also cultivates cardamom and cinchona. Nearly 2,500 families repatriated from Sri Lanka have benefited from job opportunities in TANTEA. Both the small grower and the Government sector in Tamil Nadu are beginning to realize the advantages tea possesses as a garden crop.

TANTEA has brought fame to the country by planting extensive areas with clonal plants and is ranked among the top few large clonal holdings in the world. Owning 3346 Ha of tea plantations in the Nilgiris, it is the largest individual holding in the district. The plantations done by TANTEA during 1968-79 were raised by clearing forest growth in about 185 Ha to rehabilitate repatriates from Sri Lanka. Another 591 Ha was added during 1978-81 in the grass lands of Wynaad. Addition of 337 Ha in 1982-84 was also in the grasslands of Wynaad taken over by the Forest Department under the Jenmam Abolition Act. The most recent addition of 568 Ha was made by diverting lands of the department from cultivation of other crops like Geranium, Cinchona, etc.[7]

INCOSERVE

TEA is the mainstay of the economy of the Nilgiris. There are many big Tea Estates run on commercial basis by Private Companies. Apart from these big estates the special feature of the Nilgiris is the existence of small tea gardens ranging from 1 acre to 5 acres owned by individual small/marginal farmers. There are about 30,000 small tea growers holding tea gardens to the extent of 40,000 acres.

These small tea growers are economically weak and as such they are not in a position to follow modern practices of tea cultivation and get the maximum economic benefits thereof. Individually they are not in a position to establish tea factories on their own to process green tea leaves of their garden into made tea and market the tea to their best advantage. About 30 years ago the small/marginal tea growers were totally dependent upon the Private Bought Leaf Factories. Then green tea leaves of the small tea growers were sold to these private factories at very low rates. Further the small tea growers did not have a ready market for their entire green tea leaves, particularly in rush seasons.

In order to help the small growers, the first Industrial Co-operative Tea Factory was set up in 1963 at Kundah. This experiment provided a great success and hence there was demand for organizing more Industrial Co-operative Tea Factories from the small tea growers from other areas of the Nilgiris. Today there are 17 Industrial Co-operative Tea Factories with an installed capacity of over 160 lakh kgs. of made tea. The small tea growers who were getting very low prices for their green leaves are now getting good price. Some select indicators, showing the growth of the Industrial Co-operative Tea Factories are given in Table 6.6.

TABLE – 6.6

GROWTH OF INDUSTRIAL CO-OPERATIVE TEA FACTORIES

Sl. No.	*Details*	*1963-64*	*1993-94*	*1994-95*	*1995-96*	*1996-97*
1	No. of Members	128	15,400	17,600	17,700	18,671
2	Acreage(Acres)	650	27,000	30,000	30,200	31,365
3	Quantity of Green Leaves purchased (in lakhs kgs)	5.00	498	457	502.00	563.71
4	Quantity of made tea produced (in lakhs kgs)	1.32	127	119	129.00	142.98
5	Rate paid for green tea leaves	0.80	6.86	4.44	7.66	6.60
6	Tea sales (in lakhs kgs)	1.35	126	122	135.45	138.68
7	Value of tea sales(Rs. in lakhs)	7.00	4,647	3,406	5395.30	5236.49

Source: INCOSERVE, 1997, 'Short notes on performance', p.4.

From the above figures it may be seen that increase in the last 30 years in production is more than 90 times and in sales value, more than 700 times. All the 17 Industrial Co-operative Tea Factories are being served by the Central Organization called INCOSERVE. Today the INCOSERVE and Industrial Co-operative Tea Factories are the largest producers and sellers of tea in Nilgiris commanding 16 per cent of total production. The INCOSERVE provides various services to the Industrial Co-operative Tea Factories such as warehousing of teas in the various auction centers at Coonoor, Coimbatore and Cochin, supply of fertilizers, supply of jute bags for packing tea, supply of machinery spares, diesel and other inputs to the small tea grower/members besides helping to market the teas of the factories to their best advantage[8].

Evaluation of Tea Board Schemes

Crop diversification scheme of the Tea Board for small Tea growers in South India, have been evaluated in 1996 by the Department of Agricultural Economics, Tamil Nadu Agricultural University for the Tea Board of India, Calcutta . The observations of Tamil Nadu Agricultural University are as follows:

The objectives of the scheme was to cover in the year 1989-90 around 20 to 50 hectares of the existing potato/ vegetable growing land located at higher elevation in the village/villages situated in the Nilgiris as per availability of land into tea for increasing tea production, preventing soil erosion associated with existing cultivation and generally improving the livelihood of cultivators over a period of five years.

In order to provide a further thrust for realizing the desirable objective in a planned manner, the Board introduced a scheme for the supply of essential inputs like planting materials, fertilizers, chemicals for weed and pest control in addition to making available institutional finance on easier terms.

Based on Sample studies, the report has estimated that conversion from potato to Tea causes negative net turns of Rs. 25,849 and 2,641 per ha in the first two years. From the third year, a positive return of Rs. 10,933/- ha occurs. This increases to Rs. 33,707 and 54,962 in the fourth and fifth years .

Apart from higher return of the replacing crops, the diversification is also influenced by the instability or risks involved in yield and price. The study has analysed changes in area, productivity and price of potato and tea for the period 1981-82 to 1992-93. Annual variation of area, yield and price of potato are presented in Table 6.7. Similar figures for Tea are presented in Table 6.8. The study found that potato area steadily declined from 7736 ha to 2867 ha.

TABLE - 6.7

AREA, YIELD AND PRICE OF POTATO IN NILGIRIS DISTRICT DURING 1981-82 TO 1992-93

Sl. No.	*Year*	*Area(Ha)*	*Yield (Tonnes/ha)*	*Price (Rs. /Kg)*
1	1981-82	7736	10.00	1.66
2	1982-83	6900	11.25	2.02
3	1983-84	6939	12.00	1.74
4	1984-85	7042	14.99	1.70
5	1985-86	5594	13.46	2.30
6	1986-87	5609	14.15	2.95
7	1987-88	5882	14.72	2.45
8	1988-89	4555	15.74	3.09
9	1989-90	6442	16.84	3.74
10	1990-91	3331	18.01	3.85
11	1991-92	2659	19.26	3.94
12	1992-93	2867	20.60	4.04

Source: TNAU 1996, Evaluation study p.169.

TABLE – 6.8
AREA, YIELD AND PRICE OF TEA IN NILGIRIS DISTRICT DURING 1981-82 TO 1992-93

Sl. No.	Year	Area(Ha)	Yield (Kg/ha)	Price (Rs. /Kg)
1	1981-82	24,878	1758	1.76
2	1982-83	24,861	1782	2.59
3	1983-84	24,792	2221	4.29
4	1984-85	24,910	2163	4.89
5	1985-86	25,823	2134	2.46
6	1986-87	25,881	2126	3.20
7	1987-88	25,920	2812	3.20
8	1988-89	25,827	2737	3.11
9	1989-90	26,327	2917	6.79
10	1990-91	26,260	3225	6.86
11	1991-92	36,298	2785	4.36
12	1992-93	26,350	2923	5.47

Source: TNAU (1996), Evaluation study, Page-171

The study found that the tea area had increased steadily from 24878 to 26350 ha during the years 1981 to 1993. The average yield per ha increased steadily during the period from 1758 to 2923 Kg. Per ha. Price per Kg. of tea-leaves increased during 1981-85 from Rs. 1.76 to Rs. 4.89 per Kg. There was a slump in 1986 to Rs. 2.46 per Kg. It increased again thereafter every year till it reached Rs. 6.86 per Kg. in 1991. The price declined again to Rs. 4.36 in 1992 and picked up to reach Rs. 5.47 in 1993. The study notes that constant increase in productivity coupled with rise in price of tea might have contributed to the increase in area. The economies of tea might have attracted diversification to tea from potato.

Additional income obtained from tea contributed for the betterment of the life of the beneficiaries and in asset creation. More than 50 per cent of beneficiaries felt that there was an improvement in their food consumption, clothing, education, health and participation in social activities. Most of them had invested the additional income in modernization of their houses.

Crop diversification also resulted in appreciation in land value to about three times more than the value of potato land besides generating regular employment for two men per day throughout the year. In addition, the prunings of tea and shade tree loppings were used as fuel which reduced the fuel bill for the family. Nearly 20 new bought leaf factories and three industrial cooperative tea factories were also established during last one decade. Further tea provided an effective barrier to soil erosion and helped in restoring the ecological sustainability besides providing aesthetic appearance.

Two important reasons for switching over to tea attributed by beneficiaries were un-remunerative price for vegetables and rising cost of cultivation. Despite the rise in potato price during the last 13 years (1981-82 to 1992-93) it had not compensated the increase in price of inputs. Other important reasons attributed by the beneficiaries were soil erosion, erratic rainfall, incidence of pests and diseases, animal menace and lack of good seed materials.

The result of the study confirmed that Crop Diversification Scheme had made significant impact on increasing the area under tea and production and profitability of farmers. This helped in improving the standard of living, employment generation, increase in land value besides establishment of commercial tea nurseries, manifestation of industrial activities and restoration of ecological balance.

Evaluation of HADP Tea Schemes

The Director of Evaluation and Applied Research, Government of Tamil Nadu conducted an evaluation of Hill Area Development Programme schemes providing assistance to Tea[9] in 1990. He conducted a repeat[10] study in 1995. The reports are based on data furnished by the Joint Director of Horticulture, Nilgiris District, Season and Crop reports of the Director of Statistics and reports of INCOSERVE. Some observations in the report are relevant to our study.

Hill Area Development Programme has been placing a lot of emphasis on conversion of lands from cultivation of annual vegetable crops to cultivation of Tea as a measure to reduce soil erosion in the Nilgiris. Schemes pertinent to tea cut across three sectors viz., Agricultural Engineering, Horticulture and INDCO Factories sectors. Though forming part of three district sectors, an element of vertical integration is discernible among them when an analysis of the activities included under each such sector is made. The Agricultural Engineering Department when approached takes up preliminary works in the selected farmers fields before they are developed into tea gardens. The Horticulture Department helps the selected farmers to establish new tea gardens or additional tea gardens. The INCOSERVE helps to absorb the green leaves after the tea gardens are well established and start producing green leaves.

The construction of contour bunding and staggered trenching – a condition precedent to raising a tea garden is carried out both by Agricultural Engineering Department and by the farmers themselves with the guidance of Horticulture Department.

The production of planting materials needed for raising tea in new/additional area and for infilling, the selection of tea farmers, the distribution of planting materials and other input planting advice to the farmers, dissemination of information about scientific methods of cultivation to raise tea garden are all undertaken by Horticulture Department. Vegetatively propagated Tea clones (VP clones), Fertilizers, Plant protection material and Chemicals (PPM Chemicals) and implements are distributed at subsidized prices by the Horticulture department to eligible small farmers.

The task of absorbing green leaves produced from the tea gardens covered by Horticulture Department is assigned to industry (INDCO Factory) Sector. To enable the tea grower members of the Co-operative Tea Factory to continue to remain in the new found avocations permanently. Planting materials for infilling (after pruning), inputs like fertilizers, plant protection chemicals, sprayers are supplied by subsidized rates by the INDCO factories from the funds of HADP. To absorb in full, the resultant increased production of green leaves, the installed capacity of the INDCO factory needs to be stepped up. This is done by providing loan/funds under HADP for purchase of additional machinery, replacement of old machinery, starting of new INDCO factories, establishing leaf sheds, etc. Besides, to keep the industries running on an even keel, the HADP fund is extended to INCOSERVE in the form of some common facilities like common workshops, etc. which seek to undertake speedy repairs to the machinery without holding up the production in the factory and in the process of enabling the factory to reduce considerably the repair cost which was time consuming and costlier in the past.

Thus, the integrated system provides for a three tier assistance under HADP for tea with a view to directly helping (i) in the increase in the area under tea as well as in the increase in the production of green leaves; (ii) in the absorption of entire green leaves at attractive prices; (iii) in the assurance of good marketing support for the made tea and (iv) in the restoration of ecological balance by enlarging permanent green cover which helps to minimize soil erosion.

The Horticulture Department had suggested tea crops to be raised in slopes between 10 to 30 per cent, vegetables in slopes below 10 per cent and trees in slopes above 30 per cent.

The conversion of annual crops into perennial crops is expected to serve two functions:

(i) enhancing the per unit yields of land in the short run – the yield of tea crop in the same unit of land gives more durable income than the yield obtained in the same unit of land from vegetable crops; and

(ii) minimizing soil erosion in the long run with the help of the canopy of tea crops which prevent the rains from directly hitting the ground – the primary reason identified to cause erosion.

Schemes relating to tea implemented by Horticulture Department constitute about 75 per cent of all schemes relating to tea and 19 per cent of all sectoral programmes included under HADP.

The schemes under HADP helped to replace as much as 86 per cent of the vegetable areas into tea garden which is a welcome sign. However the department had selected in certain cases, prohibited area above 30 per cent slope.

Out of every six acres claimed under tea cultivation by Horticulture Department, what was available on ground was only 5 acres.

Schemes implemented by Industry (INDCO Factory – INCOSERVE) constituted 25 per cent of all schemes relating to tea and about 6 per cent of all sectoral programmes included under HADP.

The installation of machineries supplied to INDCO factories helped in the increased capacity utilization barring Karumbalam INDCO factory which suffered failure on account of many other causes.

The total assistance under Hill Area Development Programme (HADP) to schemes relating to Tea till 1992-93 amounted to Rs. 8.71 crores, out of which Rs. 7.03 crores was meant for supply of subsidized inputs including V.P.

Clones and Rs. 1.68 crores was meant for the purpose of modernizing the infrastructure facilities in the INDCO Tea factories. The Factories utilized these funds for the purchase of CTC machinery (56 per cent of total assistance) and other accessories which were meant to quicken the process of making tea.

Upto 1992-93, 63 per cent of the potential area, i.e. 3832 ha. was brought under tea, out of 6000 ha., estimated to be the potential area for tea.

The reported area under tea was not consistent with the distribution of V.P. Clone. In 1984-85 and in 1986-87 the area reported under tea was less than the area estimated based on actual clonal distribution. Likewise between 1988-89 and 1991-92 also such a feature was observed.

A serious limitation in identifying persons with ownership of specific lands was the prevailing practice of issuing certificates of ownership rights on the basis of joint patta held by two or more persons.

Tea grower farmers also indulged in reporting higher than the actual area under tea. Tea growers resort to this kind of practice to get large input assistance from factories.

Tea growers owning 10 acres and above were also found to get the benefit meant for farmers owning upto 5 acres.

A clear shift in the pattern of cropping in the Nilgiris has taken place. Increase in perennial crops and a marked decline in annual crops is evident.

The area under perennial crop has risen from 36258 ha. in 1984-85 to 43100 ha. in 1991-92 providing an increase of 19.2 per cent. The increase in the area under tea between 1984-85 and 1991-92 works out to 35 per cent.

Summary and Research Focus

Tea which made its first appearance in the Nilgiris about 150 years ago has now become the major crop of the district. High productivity and high percentage of small growers characterize the tea-scene of the Nilgiris. Area under tea cultivation has increased in a spectacular manner after HADP was introduced in the district. UPASI and Tea Board have also put in large scale efforts to promote tea cultivation in the district. TANTEA, a public sector corporation of the Government of Tamil Nadu has converted a substantial area of forest into Tea. INCOSERVE, a federation of industrial cooperative societies of tea growers has done yeoman service in organizing small growers and assisting them. All these agencies, in addition to HADP have played significant roles in promoting tea cultivation, though with different objectives. In this context, it is interesting to take up a study to quantify the contribution of HADP in the growth of tea area in the Nilgiris. Hence this research study is taken up with the following objectives.

1. Identify the size profile of small farmers who have switched from other crops to tea cultivation.
2. Identify the crops, which were substituted by tea
3. Estimate the role of good tea prices in motivating the shift to tea.
4. Test awareness among tea farmers regarding ecological benefit of tea cultivation.
5. Estimate the segment of small tea farmers, who have availed of assistance from HADP tea scheme.
6. Compare the roles of HADP assistance and tea price as factors motivating the shift to tea cultivation.
7. Quantify the role of HADP in bringing about substitution of seasonal crop by tea.

References

1. Tea Board (1995), 'Tea Statistics 1993-94', Tea Board, Calcutta, pp. 5-16.

2. UPASI, (1997), 'Importance of Plantation Crops in South India', United Planters' Association of South India, Coonoor, pp. 1-8.

3. Muthiah. S. (1993), 'A Planting Century, the first hundred years of the United Planters' Association of South India', Affiliated East West press, Chennai-113, pp. 27-35.

4. UPASI (1995), 'The Planters Voice', September 1995, United Planters' Association of South India , Coonoor, pp. 5-7.

5. Roy Choudhury. A. (1997), *'A note on Tea Board financial assistance schemes for the development of small tea growers sector in South India'*, pp. 1-8.

6. TNAU (1996), 'An evaluation study on the impact of Small Tea Growers' Development Schemes of Tea Board in South India', *Department of Agricultural Economics, Tamil Nadu Agricultural. University, Coimbatore, meleline, pp. 223-243.*

7. TANTEA (1998), *'A Note on the growth and activities of TANTEA'*, Tamil Nadu Tea Plantation Corporation, Coonoor, pp. 1-8.

8. INCOSERVE (1997), 'Short notes on the performance of Industrial Co-operative Tea Factories and INCOSERVE in the Nilgiris District', INCOSERVE, Coonoor, pp. 1-16.

9. DEAR (1990), *'Evaluation report on schemes for providing assistance to tea growers with special reference to modernization of tea factories under HADP'*. Department

of Evaluation and Applied Research, Government of Tamil Nadu, Chennai, pp. 1-80.

10. DEAR (1995), *'Report Evaluation Study on schemes for providing assistance to tea growers with special reference to modernization of tea factories under HADP'*, Department of Evaluation and Applied Research, Government of Tamil Nadu, Chennai, pp. 1-24.

7

Analytical Study of the Role of HADP in Promoting Tea Cultivation

Introduction

Hill Area Development Programme has spent considerable sums on soil conservation. A part of this helps tea farmers in preparing their land for tea cultivation. HADP expenditure on horticulture is mainly for maintenance of tea nurseries to raise tea-clones which are distributed at a subsidized rate to small farmers. Some of the expenditure is also towards distribution of fertilizers and chemicals to tea farmers at a subsidized rate. In addition, HADP has funded development of INDCO tea factories, which provide marketing support to small tea farmers. Expenditure on these three sectors during the years 1986-97 is shown in Table 7.1. This expenditure can be regarded as the annual tea-related expenditure by HADP during these years.

It can be postulated that expenditure by HADP under the three sectors – Soil conservation, Horticulture and INDCO tea factories has resulted in increase of area under tea.

TABLE – 7.1
YEAR WISE HADP EXPENDITURE TEA PRICE, POTATO PRICE AND TEA AREA – 1982-83 TO 1997-98

S.No.	Year	Tea Price Rs/Kg X_a	HADP Exp on Tea Rs. Lakhs Y_a	Potato price Rs/Kg	Tea Area Ha T_a	Tea Area Next Year T_{a+1}
1	82-83	2.59	183.19	2.15	26362	27314
2	83-84	4.29	181.93	2.67	27314	28709
3	84-85	4.89	237.35	2.96	28709	28804
4	85-86	2.46	226.5	3.12	28804	38454
5	86-87	3.2	187.77	3.78	38454	40259
6	87-88	3.2	277.9	4.56	40259	40847
7	88-89	3.11	378.25	4.76	40847	42607
8	89-90	6.79	435.22	5.12	42607	45043
9	90-91	6.86	429.08	5.17	45043	45974
10	91-92	4.36	471.38	5.08	45974	46619
11	92-93	5.47	480.89	5.88	46619	46649
12	93-94	6.86	835.16	6.00	46649	47903
13	94-95	4.44	691.11	7.68	47903	47930
14	95-96	7.66	703.42	9.5	47930	48954
15	96-97	6.6	576.26	9.33	48954	
16	97-98	9.78	638.71	11.83		

It is also reasonable to expect that good price fetched by tea-leaves encourages farmers to take up tea-cultivation. Hence, the following hypotheses are formulated.

1. There is a positive linear correlation between expenditure by HADP on tea-related schemes and the area under cultivation.

2. There is a positive linear correlation between tea-leaf price and the area under tea cultivation.

The above hypotheses have been tested through correlation and regression as shown below.

Correlation Method

Year-wise figures for green tea leaf price (average), HADP expenditure on Tea-Schemes during the year, Tea Area and increase in area over previous year are given in Table 7.2. Correlation was tested between the following pairs.

TABLE – 7.2
YEAR WISE HADP EXPENDITURE TEA PRICE AND TEA AREA – 1982-83 TO 1997-98

S.No.	*Year*	*Tea Price Rs/Kg* X_a	*HADP Exp on Tea Rs Lakhs* Y_a	*Tea Area Ha* T_a	*Increase in area Ha* W_a
1	82-83	2.59	183.19	26362	
2	83-84	4.29	181.93	27314	952
3	84-85	4.89	237.35	28709	1395
4	85-86	2.46	226.5	28804	95
5	86-87	3.20	187.77	38454	9650
6	87-88	3.20	277.9	40259	1805
7	88-89	3.11	378.25	40847	588
8	89-90	6.79	435.22	42607	1760
9	90-91	6.86	429.08	45043	2436
10	91-92	4.36	471.38	45974	931
11	92-93	5.47	480.89	46619	645

Contd.

S.No.	Year	Tea Price Rs/Kg X_a	HADP Exp on Tea Rs Lakhs Y_a	Tea Area Ha T_a	Increase in area Ha W_a
12	93-94	6.86	835.16	46649	30
13	94-95	4.44	691.11	47903	1254
14	95-96	7.66	703.42	47930	27
15	96-97	6.6	576.26	48954	1024
16	97-98	9.78	638.71		

TABLE - 7.3
CORRELATION MATRIX

Correlation between X_a and T_a	0.669334
Correlation between X_a and T_{a+1}	0.744274
Correlation between Y_a and T_a	0.835647
Correlation between Y_a and T_{a+1}	0.893991
Correlation between Y_a and W_a	-0.660287
Correlation between Y_a and W_{a+1}	-0.285026
Correlation between X_a and W_a	-0.426193
Correlation between X_a and W_{a+1}	0.085033

(a) Tea-price and Tea Area (X_a and T_a)

(b) Tea price and Tea Area next year (X_a and $T_{(a+1)}$)

(c) Tea Related HADP Expenditure and Tea area (Y_a and T_a)

(d) Tea Related HADP Expenditure and Tea-area next year (Y_a and $T_{(a+1)}$)

(e) Tea Related HADP Expenditure and increase in tea area (Y_a and W_a)

(f) Tea Related HADP Expenditure and increase in tea area next year (Y_a and $W_{(a+1)}$)

Among all the pairs, the best correlation (R^2 = 0.89) is seen to exist between HADP Expenditure & Tea area in the next year (Y_a and $T_{(a+1)}$). It is also seen that a fair degree of correlation (R^2 = 0.74) exists between tea price and the Tea-area in the next year (X_a and $T_{(a+1)}$).

The above correlation figures validate the hypotheses that there is a positive, linear correlation between X_a and $T_{(a+1)}$ and Y_a and $T_{(a+1)}$.

Other Factors

Substitution of other crops by tea has also been encouraged by a number of other factors like un-remunerative price of potato, coffee and vegetables, incidence of pests and diseases, animal menace, lack of good seed material, steadiness of income from tea as against seasonality of income from other crops and similar other factors. The factors are numerous. For the present study they can be lumped and represented by a constant in a simple linear model.

Regression Analysis

The figures for Tea price in the year, HADP expenditure in the year, Tea area in the year and Tea-area in the next year for the period 1986-87 to 1996-97 are shown in Table 7.4. Taking index with value for the year 1986-87 = 100, indexed figures for the succeeding years were obtained as shown in the Table 7.5. The figures were used for regression analysis.

MODEL:

$$T_{a+1} = m\,X_a + b\,Y_a + p\,Z_a + q\,T_a + k$$

Where

X_a = Tea-price this year (indexed with price in 1986-87 as 100)

Y_a = HADP Expr. on Tea related schemes this year (indexed with value in 1986-87 as 100)

Z_a = Potato-price this year (indexed with value in 1986-87 as 100)

T_a = Tea-area this year (indexed with value in 1986-87 as 100) and

T_{a+1} = Tea-area next year (indexed with value in 1986-87 as 100)

m, n, p, q and k are constants

TABLE – 7.4

YEAR WISE HADP EXPENDITURE TEA LEAF PRICE, POTATO PRICE AND TEA AREA – 1982-83 TO 1997-98

Sl. No.	*Year*	*Tea Leaf Price Rs/Kg*	*HADP Exp on Tea Rs. Lakhs*	*Potato price Rs/Kg*	*Tea Area Ha*	*Tea Area Next Year*
1	82-83	2.59	183.19	2.15	26362	27314
2	83-84	4.29	181.93	2.67	27314	28709
3	84-85	4.89	237.35	2.96	28709	28804
4	85-86	2.46	226.50	3.12	28804	38454
5	86-87	3.2	187.77	3.78	38454	40259
6	87-88	3.2	277.90	4.56	40259	40847
7	88-89	3.11	378.25	4.76	40847	42607
8	89-90.	6.79	435.22	5.12	42607	45043
9	90-91	6.86	429.08	5.17	45043	45974
10	91-92	4.36	471.38	5.08	45974	46619
11	92-93	5.47	480.89	5.88	46619	46649
12	93-94	6.86	835.16	6.00	46649	47903
13	94-95	4.44	691.11	7.68	47903	47930
14	95-96	7.66	703.42	9.5	47930	48954
15	96-97	6.60	576.26	9.33	48954	
16	97-98	9.78	638.71	11.83		

TABLE – 7.5
YEAR WISE FIGURES INDEXED WITH 1986-87 VALUE = 100

Values Indexed with 1986 value = 100

Sl. No.	Year	*Tea Leaf Price*	*HADP Exp on Tea*	*Potato price*	*Tea Area*	*Tea Area Next Year*
	a	X_a	Y_a	Z_a	T_a	T_{a+1}
1	86-87	100.000	100.000	100.000	100.000	104.694
2	87-88	100.000	148.000	120.635	104.694	106.223
3	88-89	97.188	201.443	125.926	106.223	110.800
4	89-90	212.188	231.784	135.450	110.800	117.135
5	90-91	214.375	228.514	136.772	117.135	119.556
6	91-92	136.250	251.041	134.392	119.556	121.233
7	92-93	170.938	256.106	155.556	121.233	121.311
8	93-94	214.375	444.778	158.730	121.311	124.572
9	94-95	138.750	368.062	203.175	124.572	124.642
10	95-96	239.375	374.618	251.323	124.642	127.305
11	96-97	206.250	306.897	246.825	127.305	
12	97-98	305.625	340.156	312.963		

Regression Statistics

Multiple R	0.99178018
R Square	0.98362792
Adjusted R Square	0.97053026
Standard Error	1.36067198
Observations	10

ANOVA

	Df	*SS*	*MS*	*F*	*Significance F*
Regression	4	556.16538	139.0413	75.09951	0.000118637
Residual	5	9.25714	1.8514		
Total	9	565.42252			

	Coefficients	*Standard Error*	*t Stat*	*P-value*	*Lower 95%*	*Upper 95%*
Intercept	34.77157	10.18922	3.41258	0.01899	8.57938	60.96376
X Variable 1	0.025511	0.01110	2.29833	0.06992	-0.00302	0.05405
X Variable 2	0.010867	0.00887	1.22548	0.27497	-0.01193	0.03366
X Variable 3	-0.001598	0.01732	-0.09227	0.93007	-0.04612	0.04293
X Variable 4	0.662934	0.11045	6.00225	0.00184	0.37902	0.94685

Analysis. Provided by regression analysis using linear regression.

$$T_{a+1} = 0.025\,X_a + 0.011\,Y_a - 0.002\,Z_a + 0.662\,T_a + 34.771$$

Std. Error (0.011), (0.009), (0.017), (0.111), (10.189)

$R^2 = 0.984$

High value of R^2 indicates close fit between the regression line and the observed values of T_{a+1}.

From the table 7.4, the minimum value of $T_{a+1} = 104.69$. Of this, the intercept is 34.771. The variable factors account for 69.873. Thus four chosen variables account for 66.74% of the value of T_{a+1}.

Maximum value of T_{a+1} in 1995-96 = 127.31

Minimum value of T_{a+1} in 1986-87 = 104.69

Change due to operation of variables = 22.62

Hence for the above period

m(change in X_a)+ n(change in Y_a) + p(change in Z_a) + q(change in T_a) = 22.62

From the above equation and the values in the table 7.5

$(0.025 \times 139.38) + (0.011 \times 274.62) - (0.002 \times 151.32) + (0.6662 \times 24.64) = 3.485 + 3.021 - 0.309 + 16.32 = 22.509$...(A)

The observed value of the change 22.68. Hence the

calculated value is 99.24% of the observed value. The difference is due to stochastic variables.

Converting (A) to percentage of the total change:- 15.461 + 13.422 – 1.346 + 72.463 = 100

Hence 15.461% of the change is due to Tea price

13.422% of the change is due to HADP Expr.

-1.346% of the change is due to Potato price and

72.463% of the change is due to Tea area in the previous year

Tea-price and HADP expenditure have nearly equal importance (13 to 15%). Potato price has had a much lower but negative significance (-1%). As can be expected, tea-area in the next year is largely conditioned (72%) by tea area this year.

Summary

Summarizing, it can be stated that the hypotheses are proved. There is linear correlation between the values of Tea Price for the year, HADP expenditure in the year on Tea-related schemes and the Tea area in the next year for the period 1986-87 to 1996-97. Both the factors affect Tea area in a positive and significant manner.

8

Field Study

This Chapter deals with the role of HADP in shifting to tea cultivation by the small farmers. More specifically, it identifies the size profile of small farmers who have switched from other crops to tea cultivation and the crops which were substituted by tea. It also estimates the role of good tea prices in motivating the shift to tea. It tests the awareness among tea farmers regarding ecological benefit of tea cultivation and estimates the segment of small farmers who have availed the assistance from HADP tea related schemes. It compares the role of tea price and assistance provided by HADP, as factors motivating the shift to tea cultivation. Finally, it quantifies the role of HADP in bringing about substitution of seasonal crops by tea.

Sampling Procedure

The study has been taken up among small Tea farmers of the Nilgiris district. The district has about 30,000 small tea growers holding about 16,000 Ha (40,000 acres) of tea-garden. Of them, over 18,600 farmers holding over 31,000 acres are members of 17 Industrial Cooperative tea factories, located in all the six taluks of the district. Out of these 17, a selection of 11 factories was made, such that all the six taluks of the district were represented. Two factories were selected from each taluk except Gudalur, which has only one INDCO tea factory. Considering the total number of small farmers mentioned above a sample size of 531 was selected. In each factory, convenient samples of about 50 tea farmers was taken. This stratified convenient sample has representation from all taluks. The sample can be used to represent the small farmers of the Nilgiris district. However it would not be safe to draw taluk-wise inferences as the number of respondents in each taluk is small. The Respondents were interviewed using a pre-tested questionnaire. They were also asked to rank the factors which prompted them to shift from cultivation of other crops to cultivation of tea. The responses were analysed.

Profile of Respondents

Table 8.1 analyses the respondents with reference to the size of their total holdings. The figures indicate that 146 respondents each had total holding of 1 acre or less. These have been referred to as tiny farmers in subsequent tables. 134 respondents had holdings of size more than 1 but less than 2 acres. These have been referred to as marginal farmers in subsequent tables. 162 respondents had holdings of size more than 2 but less than 5 acres. These have been referred to as small farmers in subsequent tables. 89 respondents had holdings of size more than 5 acres. These have been referred to as medium farmers in subsequent tables. The definition is for convenience of presentation for this study only and is not to be taken to refer to definition of the terms by the State Government or the Tea Board. Thus it may be said Tiny, Marginal, Small and Medium farmers constitute 27 per cent, 25 per cent, 31 per cent and 17 per cent respectively of the sample.

TABLE-8.1
PROFILE OF RESPONDENT BY SIZE OF TOTAL HOLDING

Taluk	*No. of respondent holding total area* 0 - 1 acre	1.1 – 2 acres	2.1 - 5 acres	above 5 acres	*Total Numbers*
Ooty	31	33	36	7	107
Kundah	44	20	21	43	128
Coonoor	9	30	25	3	67
Kothagiri	16	14	26	23	79
Gudalur	14	9	19	8	50
Pandalur	32	28	35	5	100
TOTAL	146	134	162	89	531
Percent	27%	25%	31%	17%	100%
SIZE CLASS	Tiny	Marginal	Small	Medium	

Source: Field Survey

Table 8.2 represents similar data with reference to the area cultivated with Tea by the respondents. 44 per cent of them cultivate 1 acre or less with Tea. 26 per cent cultivate more than 1 but less than 2 ac with Tea. 30 per cent cultivate over 2 acres.

Thus 83 per cent of the respondents hold less than 5 ac. of land and 93 per cent of them cultivate tea in less than 5 ac. each. Hence, the sample represents mainly small farmers cultivating small extents of tea.

TABLE - 8.2
PROFILE OF RESPONDENTS BY AREA OF TEA-CULTIVATION

Taluk	*No. of respondents Cultivating Tea in* 0 - 1 acre	1.1 – 2 acres	2.1 - 5 acres	above 5 acres	*Total Numbers*
Ooty	46	36	22	3	107
Kundah	89	22	11	6	128
Coonoor	19	27	21	-	67

Contd.

Taluk	No. of respondents 0 - 1 acre	1.1 – 2 acres	Cultivating Tea in 2.1 - 5 acres	above 5 acres	Total Numbers
Kothagiri	25	15	25	14	79
Gudalur	17	9	21	3	50
Pandalur	41	28	11	20	100
TOTAL	237	137	111	46	531
Percent	44%	26%	21%	9%	100%

Source: Field Survey

HADP is in operation in the Nilgiris since 1974. The survey focused on those who took up tea cultivation in the last 20 years and excluded those who were cultivating tea even earlier.

Table 8.3 and 8.4 analyse the respondents by elapsed period after they took up tea cultivation. 31 per cent took up tea cultivation over 15 years ago. 38 per cent started 10 to 15 years ago. 25 per cent started 5 to 10 years ago. Only 6 per cent have converted to tea in the last five years. The rate of shift to tea cultivation reached a peak and is slowing down in the last ten years. Majority of the medium farmers converted to tea over 15 years ago. The other three categories have mainly converted during the last 5 to 15 years. Most of the conversion in Ooty, Kundah, Coonoor, Kothagiri and Pandalur taluks took place more than 10 years ago. Only in Gudalur more conversion has taken place less than 10 years ago.

TABLE - 8.3

PROFILE OF RESPONDENTS BY PERIOD SINCE CONVERSION TO TEA

Taluk-wise

Taluk	Less than 5 Years	5 to 10 Years	10 to 15 Years	More than 15 Years	Total
Ooty	2	32	44	29	107
Kundah	17	42	33	36	128

Contd.

Taluk	Less than 5 Years	5 to 10 Years	10 to 15 Years	More than 15 Years	Total
Coonoor	8	6	45	8	67
Kothagiri	2	4	19	54	79
Gudalur	3	27	11	9	50
Pandalur	0	22	47	31	100
TOTAL	32	133	199	167	531

Source: Field Survey

TABLE - 8.4
PROFILE OF RESPONDENTS BY PERIOD SINCE CONVERSION TO TEA
Size-wise

Size Class	Less than 5 Years	5 to 10 Years	10 to 15 Years	More than 15 Years	Total
Tiny	9	46	53	38	146
Marginal	7	40	50	37	134
Small	9	36	76	41	162
Medium	7	11	20	51	89
TOTAL	32	133	199	167	531
Percent	6%	25%	38%	31%	100%

Source: Field Survey

Tables 8.5 and 8.6 analyse the respondents with reference to the crop previously grown by them. The largest number (46 per cent) have shifted from Potato. Coffee (18 per cent), Vegetable other than Potato (12 per cent) and any other crop (24 per cent) accounted for, the balance.

TABLE - 8.5
PROFILE OF RESPONDENTS BY CROP WHICH FARMERS CONVERTED TO TEA

Taluk			Taluk-wise		
	Coffee	Potato	Other Veg.	Other Crop	TOTAL
Ooty	1	99	7	0	107
Kundah	35	58	16	19	128

Contd.

Taluk	*Coffee*	*Potato*	*Taluk-wise* *Other Veg.*	*Other Crop*	*TOTAL*
Coonoor	0	56	10	1	67
Kothagiri	22	30	24	3	79
Gudalur	3	0	0	47	50
Pandalur	36	1	5	58	100
TOTAL	97	244	62	128	531

Source: Field Survey

TABLE - 8.6
PROFILE OF RESPONDENTS BY CROP WHICH FARMERS CONVERTED TO TEA

Size Class	*Coffee*	*Potato*	*Size-wise* *Other Veg.*	*Other Crop*	*TOTAL*
Tiny	20	66	22	38	146
Marginal	20	74	13	27	134
Small	22	78	17	45	162
Medium	35	26	10	18	89
TOTAL	97	244	62	128	531
Percent	18%	46%	12%	24%	100

Source: Field Survey.

CROP CULTIVATED EARLIER

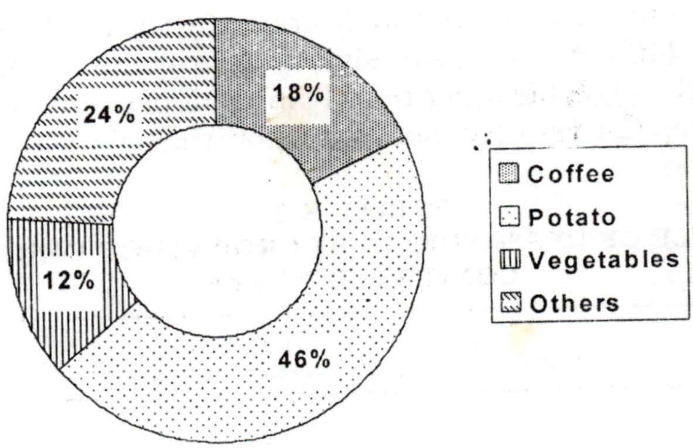

Medium farmers cultivated earlier mainly coffee or potato. The other three categories converted mainly from potato. Most of the conversion in Pandalur was from coffee. Potato was the principal crop in Ooty, Kundah and Coonoor. Nearly equal number of respondents from Kothagiri were cultivating coffee, potato or other vegetables. Respondents from Gudalur were mainly cultivating other crops.

REACH OF HADP

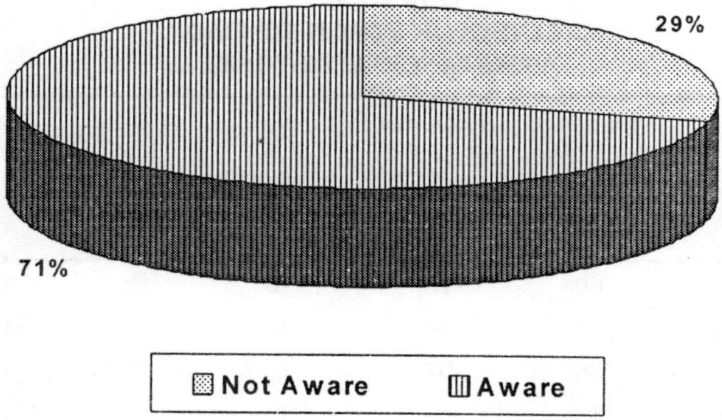

RESPONDENTS BY RECEIPT OF HADP ASSISTANCE

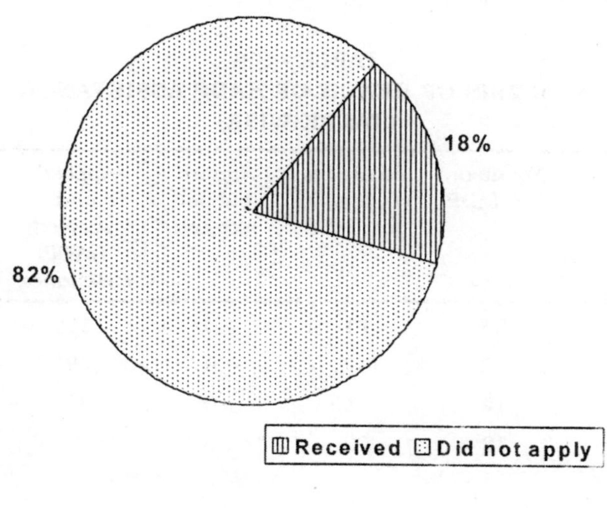

Analysis of Reach of HADP

HADP seeks to assist small farmers with total holding less than 5 ac. Tables 8.7 and 8.8 show how effective HADP was in reaching the target group in this sample. 29 per cent of the respondents were not aware that HADP provides assistance for tea-cultivation. Only 18 per cent applied for and received the assistance from HADP. A notable observation is that none who applied, failed to receive the assistance.

TABLE - 8.7
ANALYSIS OF REACH OF HADP ASSISTANCE (SIZE-WISE)

Size	*Not aware of HADP*	*Aware but not applied for HADP*	*Applied but not received*	*Applied and received HADP assistance*	*Total*
Tiny	60	73	0	13	146
Marginal	44	60	0	30	134
Small	36	97	0	29	162
Medium	13	54	0	22	89
TOTAL	153	284	0	94	531
Percent	29%	53%	0%	18%	100%

Source: Field Survey.

TABLE - 8.8
ANALYSIS OF REACH OF HADP ASSISTANCE (TALUK-WISE)

Taluk	*Not aware of HADP*	*Aware but not applied for HADP*	*Applied but not received*	*Applied and received HADP assistance*	*Total*
Ooty	35	61	0	11	107
Kundah	3	117	0	8	128
Coonoor	12	18	0	37	67
Kothagiri	12	32	0	35	79

	Not aware of HADP	*Aware but not applied for HADP*	*Applied but not received*	*Applied and received HADP assistance*	*Total*
Gudalur	6	41	0	3	50
Pandalur	85	15	0	0	100
TOTAL	153	284	0	94	531

Source: Field Survey

Among 94 who received assistance, 13 were tiny farmers (less than 1 ac. total holding), 30 were marginal farmers (1 to 2 ac) and 29 were small farmers (2 to 5 ac). As many as 22 were medium farmers who own more than 5 ac., who were not eligible for HADP assistance. Perhaps the procedures for verification of holding size were not correctly applied. In an earlier report (see Chapter 6) DEAR has commented on the difficulty in ascertaining the size of holding, due to the prevailing system of joint pattas.

The proportion of tiny farmers (0-1 ac) who have received assistance is low. However, 25 per cent of the marginal farmers (1.1 to 2 ac) have received assistance as against the overall rate of 18 per cent.

Taluk wise analysis shows that mainly respondents from Coonoor and Kothagiri have received assistance. Assistance rate is low in Ooty, Kundah and Gudalur. In Pandalur none of the 100 respondents had received assistance. Hence the 94 beneficiaries in the sample are mainly from Coonoor (37) and Kothagiri (35) with a small representation from Ooty (11). There is negligible representation from Kundah (8) and Gudalur (3) and zero representation from Pandalur.

A major observation for the purpose of the present study is that 82 per cent of those who shifted to tea-cultivation did not receive any assistance from HADP at all. They were motivated to shift to cultivation, by reasons other than assistance from HADP.

Motivation of Persons not Receiving HADP Assistance

Tables 8.9 and 8.10 analyse the motivating factor in the case of persons who did not receive HADP assistance. They were asked to state whether they were motivated by 'Good Price of tea' or by 'other reasons'. 60 per cent of the respondents said they were motivated by 'Good Tea price'. The other 40 per cent were moved by other reasons.

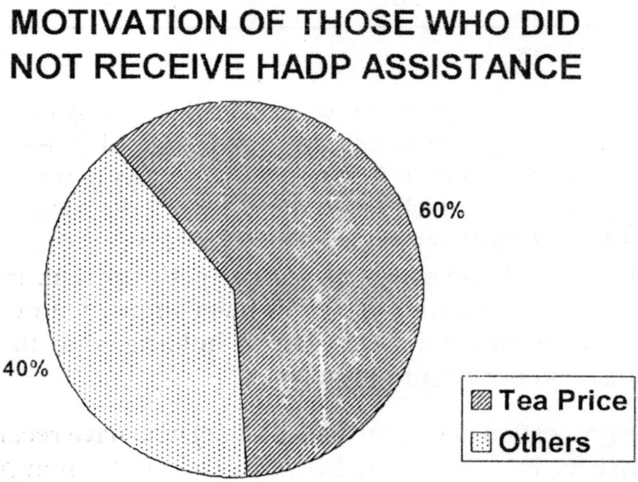

TABLE - 8.9

ANALYSIS OF RESPONSE OF THOSE WHO DID NOT RECEIVE HADP ASSISTANCE

	Number who were motivated mainly by		
Size Groups	*Tea Price*	*Other Reasons*	*Total*
Tiny	71	62	133
Marginal	63	40	103
Small	84	48	132
Medium	43	23	66
TOTAL	261	173	434
Percent	60%	40%	100%

Source: Field Survey.

TABLE - 8.10
ANALYSIS OF RESPONSE OF THOSE WHO DID NOT RECEIVE HADP ASSISTANCE

Taluks	*Number who were motivated mainly by* Tea Price	*Other Reasons*	*Total*
Ooty	63	31	94
Kundah	56	64	120
Coonoor	8	22	30
Kothagiri	15	29	44
Gudalur	20	26	46
Pandalur	99	1	100
TOTAL	261	173	434

Source: Field Survey.

All the three size groups had similar motivating factors. Practically all in Pandalur were moved by 'Good Tea Price'. It was the stronger for the two factors in Ooty taluk. In all other taluks 'other reasons' moved more farmers than 'Good Tea price'.

Awareness of the Purpose of HADP

HADP encourages Tea cultivation not for increasing tea production or with the main motive of uplifting the farmer economically. Its main objective is to reduce soil erosion by converting land from annual to perennial crop. Awareness of the purpose of HADP among the respondents was tested by asking them to indicate why they thought HADP encouraged tea cultivation. The results are displayed in Tables 8.11 and 8.12.

TABLE - 8.11
AWARENESS ABOUT PURPOSE OF HADP AMONG FARMERS SIZE-WISE

Size Class	*Not Aware*	*Aware*	*Total*
Tiny	65	81	146

Contd.

Size Class	*Not Aware*	*Aware*	*Total*
Marginal	59	75	134
Small	76	86	162
Medium	36	53	89
TOTAL	236	295	531
Percent	44%	56%	100%

Source: Field Survey.

TABLE - 8.12
AWARENESS ABOUT PURPOSE OF HADP AMONG FARMERS (TALUK-WISE)

Taluk	*Not Aware*	*Aware*	*Total*
Ooty	32	75	107
Kundah	31	97	128
Coonoor	6	61	67
Kothagiri	42	37	79
Gudalur	27	23	50
Pandalur	98	2	100
TOTAL	236	295	531

Source: Field Survey.

The figures shown that 56 per cent are aware of the correct purpose, while 44 per cent are not aware. Among Taluks, almost all respondents from Coonoor were aware, while most from Pandalur were not aware. While a majority in Kothagiri and Gudalur were not aware, majority in Ooty and Kundah were aware.

Analysis of Response of HADP Beneficiaries

Among the respondents, 94 persons were beneficiaries of HADP. They might have been motivated by HADP assistance, Good Tea price and other reasons. Since they would have been motivated by all three reasons, they were asked to rank the motivating factors in order of importance.

Based on their replies, 3 marks were awarded to the most important factor, 2 marks to the next important factor and 1 mark to the last factor.

TABLE - 8.13
RESPONSE OF BENEFICIARIES-MARKS FOR HADP ASSISTANCE SIZE-WISE

Size Group	*Number who stated HADP Assistance should be given*			*Total Number*	*Total Marks*
	3 Marks	*2 Marks*	*1 Mark*		
Tiny	0	11	1	12	23
Marginal	1	29	1	31	62
Small	2	23	3	28	55
Medium	0	22	1	23	45
TOTAL	3	85	6	94	185
Percent	3%	90%	6%	100%	

Source: Field Survey.

TABLE - 8.14
RESPONSE OF BENEFICIARIES-MARKS FOR HADP ASSISTANCE TALUK-WISE

Taluk	*Number who stated HADP Assistance should be given*			*Total Number*	*Total Marks*
	3 Marks	*2 Marks*	*1 Mark*		
Ooty	0	10	2	12	22
Kundah	1	2	3	6	10
Coonoor	2	35	0	37	76
Kothagiri	0	35	0	35	70
Gudalur	0	3	1	4	7
Pandalur	0	0	0	0	0
TOTAL	3	85	6	94	185

Source: Field Survey.

Tables 8.13 and 8.14 analyse the marks secured by HADP assistance. 90 per cent considered it the second most important reason. 6 per cent considered it the least important of the three reasons and only 3 per cent considered it the most important reason. All the respondents in Kothagiri considered it the second most important reason. In Coonoor, 2 considered it the most important reason, while 35 considered it the second most important. Following the marking system indicated, the total marks secured by this factor was 185.

TABLE - 8.15
RESPONSE OF BENEFICIARIES-MARKS FOR TEA PRICE SIZE-WISE

Size Groups	*Number who stated that Good Price should be givenTotal*			*Total*	
	3 Marks	*2 Marks*	*1 Mark*	*Number*	*Marks*
Tiny	8	0	5	13	29
Marginal	9	1	20	30	49
Small	11	3	14	28	53
Medium	21	1	1	23	66
TOTAL	49	5	40	94	197
Percent	52%	5%	42%	100%	

Source: Field Survey.

TABLE - 8.16
RESPONSE OF BENEFICIARIES-MARKS FOR TEA PRICE TALUK-WISE

Taluk	*Number who stated that Good Price should be given*			*Total*	*Total*
	3 Marks	*2 Marks*	*1 Mark*	*Number*	*Marks*
Ooty	12	0	1	13	37
Kundah	2	5	0	7	16
Coonoor	0	0	35	35	35
Kothagiri	34	0	1	35	103
Gudalur	1	0	3	4	6
Pandalur	0	0	0	0	0
TOTAL	49	5	40	94	197

Source: Field Survey.

Tables 8.15 and Table 8.16 show a similar analysis in respect of marks secured by "Good Tea Price". 62 per cent considered it the most important factor and 42 per cent considered it the least important factor. Majority of Medium and tiny farmers considered it the most important reason. In the other two categories the majority considered it the least important reason. In Coonoor taluk every one considered it the least important. But in Ooty and Kothagiri taluks almost all considered it to be the most important reason.

The wide difference in perception of the importance of Tea price is puzzling. It indicates that the perception is highly subjective.

Quantifying the responses as per the marking system "Good Tea Price" secured 197 marks.

Apart from HADP assistance and Good Tea Price, there may be many other motivating factors like non-remunerative price for coffee, potato, other crops, disease, pest attack, animal menace, difficulty in getting good seed material, steadiness of tea income as compared to seasonality of income from other crops, etc. All these have been lumped as 'other reasons' in the questionnaire.

TABLE - 8.17
RESPONSE OF BENEFICIARIES-MARKS FOR OTHER REASONS SIZE-WISE

Size Group	*Number who stated that other Reasons should be given*			*Total Number*	*Total Marks*
	3 Marks	*2 Marks*	*1 Mark*		
Tiny	5	2	6	13	25
Marginal	21	1	8	30	73
Small	17	3	9	29	66
Medium	2	0	20	22	26
TOTAL	45	6	43	94	190
Percent	48%	6%	46%	100%	

Source: Field Survey.

Tables 8.17 and 8.18 analyse the marks secured by 'other reasons'. Here also there is wide variation in perception. 48 per cent consider it the most important reason while 46 per cent consider it the least important.

TABLE - 8.18
RESPONSE OF BENEFICIARIES-MARKS FOR OTHER REASONS TALUK-WISE

Taluk	*Number who stated that other Reasons should be given*			*Total*	*Total*
	3 Marks	*2 Marks*	*1 Mark*	*Number*	*Marks*
Ooty	1	3	9	13	18
Kundah	5	0	3	8	18
Coonoor	35	2	0	37	109
Kothagiri	1	0	31	32	34
Gudalur	3	1	0	4	11
Pandalur	0	0	0	0	0
TOTAL	45	6	43	94	190

Source: Field Survey.

Most of Medium farmers consider it the least important while the majority of marginal and small farmers consider it the most important. Coonoor taluk considers it the most important, while Kothagiri considers it the least important. Thus in this factor also, very high degree of subjectivity is seen in the answers received. Awarding marks as per the scheme, this factor secures 190 marks.

Relative Importance

Total marks obtained by the three factors have been put together and displayed in Tables 8.19 and 8.20. The three factors have secured 32 per cent, 35 per cent and 33 per cent of the total marks. It shows that all the three factors secure nearly equal marks as per the respondents' perception. Tiny farmers have awarded nearly equal marks to all three categories. Marginal and small farmers have awarded marginally higher marks to 'other reasons'. Medium farmers have awarded more marks to 'Tea price'.

MOTIVATION OF HADP BENEFICIARIES

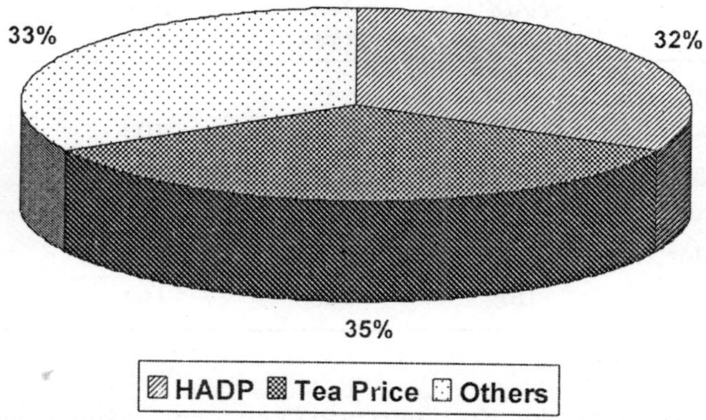

TABLE - 8.19
ANALYSIS OF RESPONSE OF HADP BENEFICIARIES

Size Group	*Total Marks for Each Motivating Factor*			
	HADP Assistance	*Tea Prices*	*Other Reasons*	*Total Marks*
Tiny	24	29	25	78
Marginal	62	50	74	186
Small	56	54	67	177
Medium	45	66	27	138
TOTAL	187	199	193	579
Percent	32%	35%	33%	100%

Source: Field Survey.

TABLE - 8.20
ANALYSIS OF RESPONSE OF HADP BENEFICIARIES TALUK-WISE

Taluk	*Total Marks for Each Motivating Factor*			
	HADP Assistance	*Tea Prices*	*Other Reasons*	*Total Marks*
Ooty	23	37	18	78

Contd.

Taluk	Total Marks for Each Motivating Factor			
	HADP Assistance	Tea Prices	Other Reasons	Total Marks
Kundah	11	16	18	45
Coonoor	76	37	109	222
Kothagiri	70	103	37	210
Gudalur	7	6	11	24
Pandalur	0	0	0	0
TOTAL	187	199	193	579

Source: Field Survey.

Among taluks, Kothagiri and Ooty farmers have awarded more marks to 'Tea Prices'. Coonoor and Gudalur farmers have awarded more marks to 'other reasons'. Kundah farmers have awarded more marks to 'other reasons'. Kundah farmers have considered all these factors almost equally important.

Summary

1. All sub-classes of small farmers are fairly represented among those who have shifted to tea cultivation. About 27 per cent have holdings of 1 acre or less. About 25 per cent hold 1.1 to 2 acres. About 31 per cent hold 2.1 to 5 acres. About 17 per cent hold more than 5 acres.

2. 44 per cent of the small farmers are cultivating tea in 1 acre or less. About 26 per cent are cultivating 1.1 to 2 acres. Another 21 per cent cultivate 2.1 to 5 acres. Only 9 per cent are cultivating tea in more than 5 acres.

3. About 31 per cent of the conversion to tea took place over 15 years ago. 38 per cent took place 10 to 15 years ago. Another 25 per cent is 5 to 10 years old. Only 6 per cent of the shift is less than 5 years old. The shift to tea cultivation seems to be slowing down.

4. 46 per cent of the farmers were growing Potato on the lands where tea is growing now. Coffee was the earlier crop in 18 per cent of the cases. Other vegetables were displaced in 12 per cent of the cases. Crops other than the above, were displaced in 24 per cent of the cases.

5. 29 percent of the small farmers are unaware that HADP provides assistance for tea cultivation. 53 per cent knew about HADP, but did not apply for assistance. Only 18 per cent applied for assistance. All those who applied, received the assistance.

6. A major observation is that 82 per cent of the farmers did not receive any assistance from HADP, 60 per cent of them were motivated by Good Tea Prices to take up tea cultivation. The other 40 per cent were motivated by other reasons.

7. Nearly half (56 per cent) of the farmers are aware of the effect of reduction in soil erosion, brought about by shifting from seasonal crops to tea. Less than half (44 per cent) are not aware of this significance.

8. Only 18 per cent of the small farmers have availed themselves of HADP assistance to shift from seasonal crops to tea. However they consider the assistance a factor only as important as 'Good Tea Price' and 'Other reasons' in motivating them to shift to tea cultivation.

9. Since only 18 per cent availed HADP assistance and even they consider it as one out of 3 equally important motivating factors, the empirical study can be said to return a finding that 6 per cent of the credit for conversion to tea, can be given to assistance provided by HADP.

9

Summary and Conclusion

The most challenging problem for our country is to provide food, health and economic security to millions of our population, without compromising ecological integrity. We need a 'Double Green Revolution' which will be as productive as the earlier green revolution, but also environmentally, friendly. This is the concept of sustainable development, which has been defined as development that meets the needs of the present, without compromising the ability of future generations to meet their own needs.

The concept of sustainability is particularly relevant to Hill areas, which have fragile ecosystems. Hills contain a diversity of valuable flora and fauna. Forests in the hill areas affect climate and rainfall of the plains also. Rivers originating in the hills provide hydel power and water for drinking and irrigation in the plains. While economic development of people living in hill areas is necessary, such development should be on sustainable lines, so that the forest and vegetative cover and variety of animal and plant life in the hills are preserved.

The Union Planning Commission has been monitoring and funding a special programme for development of selected hill districts. The programme is called the 'Hill Area Development Programme'. Guidelines for implementation of the programme have been evolved and elaborated by the Planning Commission in successive Five Year Plans.

In the State of Tamil Nadu, the HADP is being implemented in the Nilgiris District. This district is endowed with such a large diversity of flora and fauna that it has been chosen by UNESCO under its 'Man and Biosphere' programme. Its excellent climate and enchanting scenery created by lofty peaks, natural forests and grasslands attract a large number of tourists. The HADP has been implemented in this district for over two decades. The HADP in the Nilgiris pursues the goals of eco-restoration, eco-preservation and eco-development through development schemes covering many sectors of development. However, the three most important sectors are Forestry, Soil Conservation and Horticulture. Outlay on these sectors has accounted for about 54 per cent of the total outlay in recent years. Horticulture alone has accounted for over 14 per cent of the outlay.

Cultivation of vegetables and seasonal crops is practised over a considerable area of Nilgiris district. Cultivation of seasonal crops involves ploughing of the land every year. Such ploughing leads to disturbance of the top-soil. Subsequent rain tends to carry away large amounts of top-soil. Nilgiris district is witnessing a great deal of soil erosion. Many programmes have been taken up to arrest soil erosion. Among them, the most important is one of substituting seasonal crops by tea, which is a perennial crop. Once the tea bushes are established, there is no need to plough the soil. The root system of the bushes also holds the soil together and minimizes soil erosion. Hence, there is significant reduction in erosion when cultivation of a seasonal crop is substituted by cultivation of tea. For this reason, HADP has laid great emphasis on tea cultivation.

Farmers wanting to shift to tea cultivation are assisted in many ways by HADP. For contour bunding and staggered trenching of the land to suit tea cultivation, a small farmer can avail himself of schemes under Soil Conservation sector of HADP. He can obtain vegetatively propagated high yielding tea clones, fertilizers and plant protection chemicals through schemes under the Horticulture sector. HADP has also provided assistance to industrial cooperative societies of small farmers for improvement of tea factories and marketing of tea. This is booked under the INDCO tea factories sector. Thus HADP has invested in a number of schemes to promote shift from cultivation of seasonal crops to cultivation of tea. Expenditure on soil conservation, Horticulture and INDCO tea factories sectors can be regarded as tea related expenditure by HADP.

HADP is in operation in the Nilgiris district since 1975. Starting from the 1980's, there has been a steep increase in the area under tea cultivation in the district. Based on availability of reliable data, the years 1986-87 to 1996-97 have been chosen as the reference period for this study. During this period, the area under tea increased from 38,454 Ha to 48,954 Ha. During the same period annual expenditure by HADP on tea related schemes increased from Rs. 187.77 lakhs to Rs. 576.26 lakhs.

Credit has to be given to HADP for the increase in tea area mentioned above. However, there have been some other favourable factors also, which assisted to increase the area under tea. One of the important factors was the boom in tea leaf prices, which was witnessed during some years within the reference period. The price of tea leaves, which was Rs. 3.20 per Kg. in 1986-87 increased in a fluctuating manner to Rs. 6.60 in 1996-97. In-between it had touched Rs. 7.66 in 1995-96 and crossed Rs. 6.60 during the years 1989-90, 1990-91 and 1991-94. This has to be recognized as a very important factor motivating farmers to switch over to tea.

There are also other factors like steady income provided by tea for about 10 months of the year, as against one or two harvests of seasonal crops. Tea is also less prone to disease than potato and vegetable crop. Un-remunerative price fetched by potato, coffee and vegetables could have motivated some farmers to switch to tea. Menace due to animals attracted by potato could have motivated some to change over to tea. There could be other factors like promotional activity by Tea Board and UPASI.

Objectives of the Study

The purpose of the present research study is to estimate the role played by HADP in bringing about the increase in area under tea cultivation during the period 1986-87 to 1996-97.

More specifically, the objectives of the study are as follows:

1. Identify the size profile of small farmers who have switched from other corps to tea.
2. Identify the crops, which were substituted by tea.
3. Estimate the role of good tea price in motivating the shift to tea.
4. Test awareness among tea-farmers regarding ecological benefit of tea cultivation.
5. Estimate the segment of small tea farmers who have availed assistance from HADP tea scheme.
6. Compare the role of HADP assistance and tea price as factors motivating the shift to tea cultivation.
7. Quantify the role of HADP in bringing about substitution of seasonal crop by tea.

Hypothesis

1. There is a positive linear correlation between HADP and expenditure on tea related schemes during a year and the area under tea cultivation in the next year.

2. There is a positive Linear correlation between the average tea-leaf price in a year and the extent under tea cultivation in the next year.

Methodology

The required data have been collected from Primary and Secondary sources. The primary data have been collected from the respondents through a well designed, pre-tested questionnaire. The secondary data have been collected from published and unpublished sources. The collected data have been analysed using appropriate statistical tools like correlation, regression, per centage and tabular analysis.

Major Findings

1. Both tea-leaf price and tea-related HADP expenditure in a year, affect the Tea area in the next year in a significant and positive manner.

2. Tea-related expenditure by HADP can be estimated to be responsible for 12.01 per cent of the increase in tea area.

3. Good tea leaf prices can be estimated to have caused 9.6 per cent of the increase in the tea area.

4. A large part (78.39 per cent) of the increases in the tea area is due to factors other than the above.

5. All sub-classes of small farmers are fairly represented among those who have shifted to tea cultivation. About 27 per cent have holdings of 1

ac. or less. About 25 per cent hold 1.1 to 2 ac. About 31 per cent hold 2.1 to 5 ac. Only about 17 per cent hold more than 5 ac.

6. About 44 per cent of the small farmers are cultivating tea in less than 1 acre. About 26 per cent are cultivating 1 to 2 acres. Another 21 per cent are cultivating 2 to 5 acres. Only 9 per cent are cultivating tea in extents over 5 acres.

7. HADP is now over 23 years old. About 31 per cent of the conversion to tea took place over 15 years ago. 38 per cent took place 10 to 15 years ago. Another 25 per cent is 5 to 10 years old. Only 6 per cent of the shift is less than 5 years old. The shift to tea-cultivation seems to be slowing down.

8. The crop substituted by tea by 46 per cent of the farmers, is Potato. Coffee was the earlier crop in 18 per cent of the cases. Other vegetables accounted for 12 per cent of the cases. Crops other than the above were cultivated in 24 per cent of the cases.

9. Regarding reach of HADP, it is observed that 29 per cent of farmers are unaware that HADP provides assistance for tea cultivation. 53 per cent knew about HADP, but did not apply for assistance. Only 18 per cent applied for assistance. All of them received the assistance.

10. A major observation is that 82 per cent of the farmers did not receive any assistance from HADP. They were motivated by 'Good Tea Price' (60 per cent) and by 'Other reasons' (40 per cent).

11. Nearly half (56 per cent) of the farmers are aware of the effect of reduction in soil erosion, brought about by shifting from seasonal crops to Tea. Less

than half (44 per cent) are not aware of this significance.

12. Only 18 percent of the small farmers have availed themselves of HADP assistance to shift the seasonal crops to tea. However, they consider the assistance as a factor only as important as 'Good Tea Price' and 'Other reasons' in motivating their shift.

13. Since only 18 per cent availed HADP assistance and even they consider it as one cut of 3 equally important motivating factors, the empirical study returns a finding that 6 per cent of the credit for conversion to tea can be given to HADP assistance. However, the econometric study has estimated that 12 per cent of the increase in the area during 1986-87 to 1996-97 can be regarded as the result of expenditure by HADP on tea related schemes. Both the studies suffer from a number of limitations, which have been listed above. Between the two methods, the limitations of the empirical method are most severe and the results subjective.

Hence, it would be reasonable to place the final figure closer to that provided by the econometric study rather than the empirical study. On this basis, the contribution of HADP assistance to increase in tea area in the Nilgiris during the period 1986-87 to 1996-97 may be placed at 10 per cent.

Conclusion

During the years 1986-87 to 1996-97, the area under cultivation in the Nilgiris District increased from 38,454 Ha to 48,954 Ha. Out of this increase of 10,500 Ha, HADP assistance alone can be estimated to have accounted for 1050 Ha. In addition to making a contribution as above, HADP has created a good demonstration effect. It has acted as a catalyst in promoting shift from other crops to tea cultivation in a much larger area. In all about 10,500 Ha. of land which was earlier cultivated with other crops has come under tea cultivation during the period 1986-87 to 1996-97. Shifting of cultivation from seasonal crops to tea, has beneficial effect on the ecology of the district, by reduction in soil erosion. Farmers also get better economic returns through tea cultivation. Hence, HADP has played a significant role in the sustainable development of the Nilgiris District by encouraging substitution of seasonal crops with tea.

10

Tea in the Nilgiris in 2004

Some things have changed in the Nilgiris after 1999. The present situation is discussed below.

Population

Census of 2001 has revealed that the population of Tamil Nadu increased from 5.59 crores in 1991 to 6.24 crores in 2001. The population of the Nilgiris district has increased from 7.10 lakhs in 1991 to 7.65 lakhs in 2001. The population figures are given below:-

	Male	*Female*	*Total*
Rural	1,52,968	1,56,684	3,09,652
Urban	2,26,642	2,28,532	4,55,174
Total	3,79,610	3,85,216	7,64,826

Source: Statistical Hand book of Tamil Nadu, 2003

The percentage of urban population to the total is 59.65% compared to the State average of 44.04%. The sex ratio in the district is 1015 females to 1000 males as against 987 for the State as a whole. Percentage of literacy is 80.01% compared to the State average of 73.45%. The percentage of

SC/ST population out of the total is 31.23% and 3.72% as compared to State average figures of 19% and 1.04%.

Hill Area Development Programme in Nilgiris

HADP continues to be in operation in the district. At present, the main objectives of the programme are ecological preservation, restoration and overall development of district economy. Specific objectives of the programme are mentioned below:

1. To preserve and conserve extremely fragile tropical eco-system i.e., sholas and grasslands of Nilgiris.
2. Development of land use plan for forest area as well as cultivated areas on the basis of slope levels and other climatic, ecological considerations.
3. Conserve soil and water to increase productivity of the land by predominantly using vegetative methods and changing the cropping pattern.
4. Promote non-land based economic activities to uplift the poor people and to ensure environment protection.
5. Economic up-liftment of tribals in isolated locations, settlements.
6. Manage the human pressures on eco-system through comprehensive human settlement policy and discourage migration.
7. "Area based Approach" will be given top priority. Integrated plans shall be prepared for all watersheds and high priority watershed shall be chosen for treatment.
8. Use of scientific interventions will be encouraged i.e., application of Remote Sensing, etc.,
9. Promotion of Non-Conventional Energy sources i.e., Solar, Hydro, Bio-gas, etc.

HADP Outlay (Rs. in lakhs)

Name of the Sector	*Ninth Plan (1997-2002)*		*Tenth Plan (2002-2003)*		*(2003-2004)*		*(2004-2005)*	
	Outlay	*% of Total*	*Outlay*	*% of Total*	*Outlay*	*% of Total*	*Outlay*	*% of Total*
Soil Conservation	1864.87	17.36	408.03	18.46	327.79	14.83	358.01	16.20
Forestry	1800.22	16.75	355.95	16.11	287.73	13.02	369.48	16.72
Horticulture	1416.95	13.19	299.48	13.55	327.59	14.82	315.00	14.25
INDCO Tea Factories	83.00	0.77	20.00	0.91	20.00	0.91	20.00*	0.91
Others	5578.96	51.93	1126.54	50.97	1246.89	56.42	1147.51	51.92
Total	10744.00	100.00	2210.00	100.00	2210.00	100.00	2210.00	100.00

* For Revival Plan for tea-plantation area in Kundah.

Source: Annual Plan Proposals for HADP, Govt. of Tamil Nadu

The activities of HADP cover not only Forest, Soil Conservation and Horticulture as the Core sectors but also other sectors meeting the socio-economic developmental needs of the district.

The figures of outlay up to 8th Plan have been furnished in the thesis. The subsequent figures are given on page No. 185.

It may be seen that Soil conservation, Forestry and Horticulture continue to be the main thrust sectors of HADP. Assistance to INDCO Tea Factories continued till 2003-04. In the subsequent year, it was stopped and a scheme to revive tea-plantations in Kundah Taluk was introduced. Thus the tea sector continues to receive support from HADP.

Land-use pattern

The HADP Annual Plan 2004-05 gives the following data about land-use in the district and reports an increase in Forest area in the last ten years.

	Area in Hectares	*% to Total Area*
A. Total Geographical Area	254485	(100)
i. Forest	142579	(56)
ii. Barren and uncultivable land	3371	(1.3)
iii. Land put to non-agricultural use	9732	(3.8)
iv. Cultivable waste	2524	(1.1)
v. Permanent pastures and other grazing land	5133	(2.0)
vi. Miscellaneous tree crops and groves (not included in the net area sown)	3452	(1.3)
vii. Current fallow lands	4904	(1.9)
viii. Other fallow lands	3990	(1.5)
ix. Net area sown	78800	(30.9)
B. Area sown more than once	73	(Negligible)
C. Gross cropped area (GCA)	78853	(30.9)

Source: Annual Plan Proposals for HADP, Govt. of Tamil Nadu

The report gives the latest areas under Tea, Coffee and Potato as follows:

Tea	51,303 Hec.
Coffee	7,431 Hec.
Potato	3,357 Hec.

Thus tea area has increased further.

Changed fortune of Tea cultivation

India continues to be the largest producer of tea. World tea production details for the year 2002 are as under:-

Country	*Production (M Kg)*
INDIA	826
CHINA	715
SRI LANKA	310
KENYA	287
INDONESIA	167
TURKEY	145
OTHERS	572
TOTAL	3022

Source: UPASI, 2003

The tea production and export from India are as follows:-

Year	*Production (M Kg)*	*Exports (M Kg)*
1997	811	203
1998	870	210
1999	806	192
2000	846	207
2001	854	180
2002	826	198

Source: J Thomas, 2001 & UPASI, 2003

After reaching a peak of 210 million kg in 1998, Tea exports fell thereafter. Decline in exports has had its impact on price fetched by made tea in auctions as may be seen from the following:-

(Price in Rupees per Kg.)

CENTRE	1997	1998	1999
COCHIN	61.57	73.31	62.04
COIMBATORE	60.31	68.74	57.26
COONOOR	57.13	65.06	53.34
SOUTH INDIA	59.67	69.04	57.55

Source : *Mishra Committee Report, 2000*

This in turn has had its impact on the price paid for green leaf to the growers by Tea factories as may be seen from the table:-

Year	*Rs. Per Kg.*
1995-96	6.96
1996-97	6.42
1997-98	12.97
1998-99	10.36
1999-2000	7.73
April 2000	5.00

Source : *Mishra Committee Report, 2000*

Since the price for green leaf paid to the growers is linked to the market price of made tea, the small grower of Nilgiris has been realizing a price which is as low as about Rs. 5/- per kg of green leaf. Since such a low return is barely able to cover the cost of cultivation of tea and plucking of leaves, the small growers, who realized nearly Rs. 13 per kg during 1997-98 are agitated and have been representing to Government for intervention to remedy the situation.

Relief by Govt. of Tamil Nadu

Government of Tamil Nadu has taken a number of steps to assist Tea growers. Some of them are as follows:-

- Government of Tamil Nadu issued an amendment notification on 2.6.2000 reducing the sales tax from 8% to 4% under TNGST for a period of 6 months from 29.4.2001 and further extended up to 31.5.2002
- The State Government reduced General Sales Tax from 4% to 2% in respect of tea sold in auction Centres at Coonoor and Coimbatore.
- The State Government ordered sale of Dust Tea through Public Distribution System vide G.O. Ms. No.259, Co-operation Food and Consumer Protection (F1) Department, dated 20.7.2001
- The Government have issued orders to open a Tea Auction center at Coonoor as per G.O. Ms. No.36, Small Industries Department dated 16.7.2002. The auction centre has been registered on 28.8.2002.
- The Government has abolished Agricultural Income Tax.

Relief by Government of India

The Government of India and the Tea Board have also made various interventions. Some are mentioned below:-

- Central Government raised the custom duty for the tea imported from other countries from the existing level of 15% to 35% ad valorem from 4.5.2000.
- The Central Government announced a scheme for the benefit of small tea growers for giving subsidy at Rs. 1.25 per kg. of green tea leaves from 1.5.2000

to 15.7.2000, wherever the price of the made tea was less than Rs. 55 per kilo, which was subsequently increased to Rs. 2/- per kg. from 16.7.2000 to 31.10.2000.

- A major Quality Upgradation Programme for the small sector is in operation for the past two years, under which over 200 village campaigns, 40 factory-level experiments-cum-demonstrations, several seminars and extensive publicity measures have been taken up to improve the leaf standards in small tea growers' holdings and manufacturing practices in bought leaf/cooperative tea factories.
- Existing schemes of the Tea Board for replanting, rejuvenation, new area development and factory modernization have been intensified.
- Delegations of small growers have been taken to tea producing areas in North India to expose them to cultural practices in tea gardens and factories there and then enable them to improve the quality of tea-leaf produced by them.
- The system of primary marketing of teas and the post auction value chain has been studied in depth so that suitable interventions can be made to protect the legitimate interests of the industry if need be.
- To counter the decline in our exports, a medium term export strategy, called 'Tea Export Initiative' has been formulated and is now in the initial stages of implementation.
- In the short term, the Tea Board has tried to boost our export performance by introducing an Export Incentive Scheme for a limited period, under which exporters who show better performance are granted a subsidy ranging from Rs. 2 per kilogram of

orthodox tea in bulk to Rs. 10 for each kilogram of tea in tea bags. This is apart from the Board's scheme for exporters to get part reimbursement of expenditure incurred on travel abroad, participation in trade fairs or buyer-seller meets as well as promotional work.

(*Tea Board, 2003*)

Government of India also have taken note of the problems facing the plantation industry in general. A Committee was appointed by the Commerce Ministry to look into the problems. In its report the Committee (Saptharishi Committee, 2003) has made the following observations about Tea:

India is the largest producer and consumer of the tea in the world accounting for 28% of world production and 14% of the world trade. Export of tea is around 25% of the domestic production. The production of tea has risen from 835.64 million kgs to 847.25 million kgs during 1997-98 and 2001-2002, whereas the domestic consumption has risen from 602 million kgs to 679 million kgs during the same period. While the import of the tea has risen from 2.61 million kgs to 16.02 million kgs, the volume exported has fallen from 211.26 million kgs to 190.00 million kgs in the same period. The shrinking market share of a very old industry with brand equity is a case of concern. Some of the parameters indicating the health of tea industry are given below:

Year	*Index of production*	*Index of Area*	*Index of Yield*	*Yield for hectare(kg)*
1980-81	101.6	100.5	101.1	1491
1990-91	132.3	110.3	119.9	1794
2000-01	151.3	135.5	113.3	1673

Source: Saptharishi Committee, 2003

The Committee has made the following principal recommendations to improve the viability of plantations:-

- To reduce the burden on Plantations, Government of India and State Governments/Local Self-Government should agree to bear 50% of the social and infrastructural cost under the Plantations Labour Act, while the industry should bear the remaining 50% of this cost.

- The Committee is of the view that the rate of maximum marginal agricultural income tax may be reduced to the level of the maximum marginal corporate income tax/central income tax.

- The State Governments may be requested to take a holistic view and examine the taxation issues in totality and rationalize the relevant enactments keeping in mind the financial health of the plantation sector.

- In the contemporary world of competition, the product should be price competitive. It is, therefore, essential that wages should be linked to productivity in the tea, coffee or natural rubber sector.

- Since plantation crops are mass consumed items and are produced and consumed across several States, a uniform VAT at the lowest slab is recommended for the healthy growth of the industry.

(*Saptharishi Committee, 2003*)

Future

Despite the various initiatives of the Government of Tamil Nadu, Government of India and the Tea Board, the gloom in plantations has not cleared. There is an apprehension that the world supply of tea is in excess of the demand and this fundamental fact is driving down tea prices, leading to consequent effects on Plantations and small growers. However the optimists are hoping that the gloom will increase the demand for the 'cup that cheers' and thereby bring back the good old days, as it happens in business-cycles.

References

- Annual Plan Proposals of HADP, Planning Development & Special Initiatives Department, Government of Tamil Nadu, unpublished.
- J Thomas, 2001, J. Thomas & Company Private Limited, "Tea Market Annual Report and Statistics 2001"
- Mishra Committee Report, 2000, Government of Tamil Nadu, unpublished.
- Saptharishi Committee, 2003, Report of the Inter-Ministerial Committee constituted by the Ministry of Labour to look into the various issues relating to the Plantation Sector in India, Government of India, unpublished.
- Statistical Hand book of Tamil Nadu, 2003, Department of Economics and Statistics, Government of Tamil Nadu
- Tea Board, 2003, "Situation prevailing in the tea industry in South India" an article by Shri Vikram Kapur, I.A.S, Executive Director, Tea Board, unpublished.
- UPASI, 2003, The United Planters' Association of Southern India, "Emerging Trends in the Plantation Sector". September 2003.

11

The Nilgiris—A Hundred Years Ago

Madras District Gazetteer of the Nilgiris District, prepared by W. Francis ICS and published in 1908, gives a picture of the Nilgiris nearly a century ago-

"The Orange Valley! There is a perfume in the very name! Our old heart warms, and a delicious languor steals over our senses, as we recall to mind the silent, balmy incense-breathing moment when first we trod the flowery shades of that enchanting spot. It seemed to us the abode of peace and innocence, a place for young lovers to walk hand in hand, culling the golden fruit and twining into bridal wreaths the snow-white blossoms which made the very air love sick with their fragrance".

The Nilgiris hills, having a rainfall of less than 40 inches on some of the driest parts of the eastern side, and of 200 inches on the moistest parts of the western slopes, possess, as might be expected, very varied and interesting flora, exceedingly numerous in 'genera and species.'

With the exception of dense, evergreen, moist forests on the western sides, the whole area has been well explored by botanists, and it is probable that there are few plants now botanically unknown on the plateau and the deciduous forests of the slopes, which are of immense extent, very difficult to get at, and very feverish at the lower elevations; and as they contain no habitations or supplies of any sort, the visits of botanists to them have been generally of a flying nature. The trees in these tracts attain an immense size, being often 200 or 250 feet in height, so that it is no easy matter to obtain their flowers; and there can be no doubt that a good many un-described species still await the botanist. Some of the trees flower in the cold season, some in the hot weather, and some in the rains, while some few are in boom all the year round, but it is believed that the majority flower between February and the middle of May, which is the most unhealthy time of the year. The shrubs, creepers and herbaceous plants in these tracts are pretty well known, but a careful search at any season of the year, should undoubtedly be rewarded by some novelties.

The animals of the district include the elephant, tiger, leopard and Indian (sloth) bear, the sambhar, spotted, barking, four-horned, and mouse, deer, antelope, bison, pig, 'Nilgiri ibex' and wild dog, besides hares and the fast and sturdy hill jackal which is the quarry of the Ootacamund Hunt.

Elephants may be said never to visit the plateau itself now-a-days, though sixty years ago they now and then came up to the Kundah to escape the fiery heat below. Their chief haunt in the district at present is the belt of forest below the north side of the plateau (round about Masinigaudi and Anaikatti) and the Wynaad. There they are still so numerous as to be sometimes a serious nuisance to travellers and cultivators.

Tigers occur all over the district, both on the lower levels and on the plateau. They are commonest on the latter from March to June when the heat and the forest fires drive them up from below. General Douglas Hamilton mentions seeing five of them, (two full-grown and three younger ones the size of large leopards) all together on one occasion near Ounamund (apparently what is now called 'one mand') shola.

In 1903 a sportsman at Naduvattam succeeded in killing, one after the other, four which had gone down into a deep ravine after a dead pony. Not long ago one was caught in the Ouchterlony valley in a barbed wire running noose fastened to two trees; which had been set by Kurumbas for sambhar, but after terrific struggles succeeded in breaking two of the wires and getting away with the loss of a great deal of hair and blood.

Leopards, like tigers, are common in all parts of the district. So many cases of black leopards are reported that there is some ground for supposing that they are commoner on the hills than in the plains. Bears are seldom seen on the plateau itself but are frequent on the slopes in the lower country.

The Nilgiri ibex (Hemitragus hylocrius, really a wild goat) is perhaps the most interesting of the game animals of the plateau as it belongs to a strictly Indian genus the only other species in which is the tarh of the Himalayas, occurs nowhere in the world. Outside the Madras Presidency; and, with the exception of an ibex on the higher mountains of Abyssinia, is the only goat living south of the north temperate none. When Europeans first came to the hills, it was unknown to science and was commonly called 'the chamols'. It is not, as its name would imply, peculiar to the Nilgiris, but is found all along the Western Ghats southwards (including the Anaimalais and Palnis) as far as Cape Comorin. In this district it lives only on the plateau and is commonest on the precipitous southern and western sides of the Kundahs. Its arch-enemy is the leopard.

A generation before Francis, another writer has chronicled the beauty of the land in the last century as follows[2]:-

The country in which we find the Todas, though not by many moves perhaps the seat of his origin, is worthy of notice; for thus we shall better realize how man lived in days when he had advanced scarce more than one step from the period of his rude simplicity; in what style of place he gradually acquired forms and social habits, that he never forsook entirely; and how he multiplied unobserved, until his country could be longer contain his progeny – then migrated and founded nations.

Picture an abrupt-edged table-land, on the apex of a solitary mountain – a very Laputa in its complete isolation of some 7,000 ft. in altitude – whose evergreen surface is one continued intermixture of rounded hills, with tracts of rolling prairie; The hills as accessible as those of Malvern; the prairie land as ceaseless, in its long undulations, as the billows of an ocean. Short coarse grass, clothes the whole, save where the deep forest holds possession of the damp secluded valleys, or the cool little woods moss the banks of the prolonged gulleys, through which the trickling streams or dashing bourns course down the silent hill-sides; then collect, and, through successive vigorous rapids and tumultuous cataracts-where from behind the clouds of spray and mist, noise roars its prolonged approval-precipitate themselves into the plains below. Wherever, in fact, rich soil and a perennial supply of moisture may be found, there are the ever silent woods; for the periods of annual drought are long; the monsoon rain flows quickly out of the hard surface of the exposed hills; and the scorched grass containing the young saplings is yearly fired.

These woods and forests, and lovely glades, whose perfect quiet is broken only by the calls of wild animals and birds, or by the rustic sounds of Toda cattle-almost equally wild-herding in the open, form pre-eminently the characteristic features of the scenery; adding emphasis to the singularly peaceful beauty of the view.

Before the Englishman came to the Nilgiris, and colonized the Todas' land, the country was full of game; hares; peafowl, partridge, jungle fowl, and numerous small birds, filled the secluded woods; deer or sorts, bison, and jungle-sheep roamed their open pastures, the tiger and leopard were common; and packs of the wild dog – Chennai – running, mute, hunted the largest deer with the unerring certainty of fate.

The Toda buffalos, half-wide, had learnt to defend themselves and their young by tactics, the offspring of their bravery and skill; forming a rough triangular phalanx, with the courageous and strong bulls at apex and flanks, and the females and young in the hollow of the base, they would face the common enemy, and charging him in a body, gore and trample him under foot. The Todas, confident in the prowess of these animals, leave them to be herded by mere striplings armed with light wands; knowing that the animals and the children under their protection, would be perfectly safe[2].

Francis's Gazetteer gives us information about the development of the district since the turn of 19th century.

Early history:- The Nilgiris district may almost be said to be one of those happy countries which have no history. Even had it been sufficiently rich or strategically important to tempt an invader, its inhospitable climate, the difficulties of the passes up to it and the feverish jungle which hedged it round would have deterred any but the boldest. But it never contained any towns worth sacking or forts worth capture; and the only inhabitants were poor graziers and cultivators. Consequently the rapacious rulers round about almost disregarded it. For this and other reasons, the materials for an account of its people in the days preceding the British occupation are very meager.

The Mysore Wars so well known in history were waged by the East India Company against Haidar Ali and his son Tipu in the endeavor to cripple their power; and the Third Mysore war ended at length in victory; Srirangapatnam being captured in 1799 and Tipu killed during the final assault. In the treaty which followed (settling the division, between the Company and its allies, of Tipu's territories) the Nilgiri plateau, which was included in the 'Danaigincotah' district (revenue 35,000 Kantiraya pagodas) mentioned in the schedule thereto, was ceded to the Company.

Though a number of expeditions were sent by the English Administration in Coimbatore, to study the newly ceded area, it was not until the 1820's that the real beauty and climate of the territory was noticed and appreciated by senior English officers. According to Francis, much credit for this goes to Mr. John Sullivan, Collector of Coimbatore, Sir Thomas Monroe and Mr. S.R.Lushington, Governors of Madras. Their efforts made the Government take up development of Ootacamund as a sanatorium for sick and retired officers.

It must be remembered that there were then no hill-stations in India, and that officials who were broken in health by the climate of the plains used to travel all the way to the Cape or Mauritius (both altogether inferior, climatically, to the Nilgiris) to recoup. The possibility of there existing in South India, close to the equator, a region where the climate was cool and invigorating enough not only to restore invalids to health but to induce retired officials to settle down in it was at that time to most people absolutely incredible. Lieutenant Burton says that when the first visitors to the hills stated that the thermometer there was 25 degrees lower than on the plains such a climate within the tropics was considered so great an anomaly that few would believe in its existence.

A report of September 1827 by Mr. Sullivan, sums up the progress made upto then at Ootacamund. Roads have been made in all directions about the settlement so that invalids may take either horse or palanquin exercise with almost as much facility as in the low country. A fine piece of water has also been constructed, on which boats are beginning to ply. A subscription has been set on foot for a public reading room.

Ootacamund, in short, was gradually approximating to a state of comfort and civilization.

Though succeeding Governors evinced a less personal and enthusiastic interest in the Nilgiris than had been shown by Mr. Lushington, the advantages of the hills were now so widely known and appreciated that they progressed rapidly none the less.

Lord Elphinstone became Governor in 1837, and during his rule the hills first began to be opened up for coffee estates.

In 1868, the Nilgiris district was separated from Coimbatore and placed under a Commissioner with revenue, criminal and civil jurisdiction.

In 1882, the district was put under the same footing as others, and a Collector was appointed. Francis's Gazetter gives us an idea of the land-use prevailing in the Nilgiris in the early years of the present century. The Gazetteer also talks of the rise and decline of coffee cultivation and mentions a brief 'gold-rush' that excited the district and caused distraction to the plantation industry. The minor mention accorded to tea, contracts with the present dominant position of the crop.

AGRICULTURE in the district divides itself naturally into two classes; namely, the cultivation of food-crops carried out by the natives and the growth by Europeans of special products such as coffee, tea, cinchona, rubber, fruit, etc. The following statistics show at a glance the general agricultural position in the district.

Percentage of the area shown in the village accounts which is

Taluk	*Forest & other Area not available for cultivation*	*Cultivable waste other than fallow*	*Current fallows*	*Net Area Cropped*
Coonoor	42.8	7.2	29.6	20.4
Ootacamund	80.4	1.3	10.7	7.6
Gudalur	38.6	22.3	29.5	9.6
District total	58.8	8.9	20.9	11.4

Percentage of the area under each crop to total area cropped

Sammi	14.7	4.3	2.3	8.4
Rice	-	-	33.1	7.8
Korali	11.9	7.8	-	7.7
Ragi	1.5	7.1	4.4	4.0
Barley	5.4	3.4	-	3.5
Wheat	1.7	2.9	-	1.7
Others	1.2	20.0	-	7.0
Oil-seeds	-	0.7	-	0.2
Condiments & Spices	0.3	0.2	0.1	0.2
Coffee	44.6	18.1	43.9	36.0
Tea	7.7	12.8	13.1	10.6
Cinchona	1.1	10.9	2.6	4.6
Potato	4.8	3.2	-	3.2
Others	0.4	0.7	0.4	0.5
Blue Gum	4.5	7.9	-	4.5
Others	0.2	-	-	-

From these it will be seen that in Coonoor taluk only half the area shown in the village accounts is cropped or under fallows, while seven per cent of its culturable land is still unoccupied and the remainder is forest or other land not available for cultivation; that in Ootacamund, less than a fifth of the total area is cropped or fallow and hardly any unoccupied land remains, since four-fifths of the taluk is forest or other land not available for cultivation; and that in Gudalur, the forests and occupied land each make up some two-fifths of the total area while as much as one-fifth is culturable but not occupied.

Again, in Coonoor, of the total area cropped, more than half is grown with coffee, tea and cinchona, while the chief cereals are the two millets called samai (Panicum miliare) and korali (Setaria glauca), which are often sown together in the same field; in Ootacamund, the area under plantation products is proportionately smaller, while korali and ragi (Eleusina coracana) are the principal food-crops; and in Gudalur the percentage under coffee, tea, etc., is higher than in either of the other taluks, but the chief (indeed almost the only) cereal is paddy. The area shown under plantations in this last taluk, however, includes a good many estates which have now been practically abandoned. In both Coonoor and Ootacamund the areas planted with blue gum trees for firewood are considerable.

Coffee

The world's consumption of coffee is estimated at about sixteen million bags; and of this about twelve million bags are supplied by Brazil and the remaining four million by Java and South India. In South India more than half the coffee producing area is situated in Mysore and the remainder in the Madras Presidency, Coorg and Travancore. According to the official returns, the area in the Nilgiris is now 26,000 acres; but the figures for this product are based for the most part on the planters' own reports, and as these are too often neither complete nor regularly forwarded, the statistics are seldom really trustworthy.

The plant appears to have been introduced into the Malabar Wynaad from Anjarakandi by Mr. Brown in 1828, but it was not until 1839 that its cultivation became an enterprise there. The first plantations on the Nilgiri plateau were started about the same time.

According to the statistics (which, however, as already stated, require to be accepted with reserve) the industry reached its highest point of prosperity in 1878, when the area cultivated in the whole district was 25,000 acres and the crop reached 10 ¼ million pounds. Insect pests and disease in the plantations, low prices resulting from increased production in other countries, and the dissipation of much energy in the vain search for gold in the Wynaad of 1879-82 caused a reaction: and in 1883-84 the exports were 3 per cent less, prices in London having dropped from between pounds 3-5-0 and 4 pound a cwt. to between pounds 2-15-6 and pounds 2-19-0. Short crops in Brazil and speculation in the European and American markets occasioned a recovery in prices in the years following, and by 1890 they had risen to pounds 4-49-0 a cwt.

Various diseases, however, had ruined many estates, and the exports, instead of rising in consequence of better prices, began to fall. In 1892-93 prices still kept up owing to the facts that the coffee in Ceylon had been so attacked by various pests that large areas of it had been abandoned, and that the crops in Java and Brazil were small. In 1893-94 the sustained operations of a French syndicate, aided by a series of revolutions (in 1889, 1891 and 1893) in Brazil and a short crop in Java, resulted in the high level being maintained; but in 1896-97 the Brazilian crop was splendid and the Indian one short, and prices declined sharply. In the next few years over-production in Brazil caused a further fall in all coffees of the classes which (like the Indian sorts) compared with the product of that country and were not a grade superior to it, and this downward movement continued until 1900, when the low water-mark was reached and the average price of Indian plantation coffee was only pounds 2-7-0 a cwt. – a decline of 50 per cent on the figure of 1897.

Disease, however, was now doing much less damage than before, and in 1900-1901 exports began to rise in spite of the low prices realized. This rise has steadily continued up to date, and the quantity exported from the Presidency in 1905-06 (349,000 cwts.) was 45 per cent higher than the figure for 1900-01 and the value (171 lakhs) greater than in any year except one, since 1895-96.

It is only however by rigid economy and constant care that coffee estates now pay, and the industry is anything but a flourishing condition; Scores of plantations in the Wynaad have been entirely abandoned and relapsed into jungle, and others are in the hands of natives who merely pick such crop as the trees will give with the minimum of cultivation.

Tea

Of the tea exported from India only a very small quantity is grown in South India, and even of this latter amount, the proportion raised in the Nilgiris is at present less than one-half per cent. The area under tea in the district is reported to be about 8,000 acres, but these figures, like those for coffee, require to be accepted with reserve since planters are irregular in sending in their returns. The area is undoubtedly increasing rapidly, however, as tea is less liable than coffee to diseases and pests and its price has not yet suffered to the same extent from over-production, so that in many cases it has been planted on estates on which coffee had provided a failure.

The history of the cultivation of tea in the district dates from 1833. However, many attempts failed before Tea estate became economical. Even by 1869, only 200-300 acres had been planted with Tea. The area expanded thereafter.

The Gazetteer contains an account of the attempts made in the 19th century to protect forests in the district. It is interesting to see that destruction of forests was noted with concern in 1908 also and blame was placed on previous occupants. The Gazetteer records:

The Sholas on the plateau, are not of any great importance from a commercial point of view, as the trees in them are slow-growing varieties (largely Eagenias and rhododendron) which produce timber of little or no value and probably take at least a century to mature; but they add greatly to the beauty of the country and are of immense use in protecting sources of water-supply.

There can be little doubt that throughout the country now occupied by the Badagas these sholas were formerly far more numerous and extensive than at present, and that the Badagas had done immense destruction among them even before the first Europeans came to the hills.

Many steams which were once perennial are now, owing to the absence of forests which might absorb rainfall, quite dry one day and raging torrents the next, and that the amount of scour they occasion when in these sudden floods is a danger to cultivation, roads and bridges.

When Europeans first settled on the plateau the great demand for firewood and building material resulted in much reckless felling of the sholas near Ootacamund and Coonoor, and Government made early efforts to check the mischief. They inserted a clause in the title-deeds of land granted by them requiring the grantee to plant a sapling for every tree he felled; and in 1837 they directed that in future no trees should be cut down within the military limits of Ootacamund without special sanctions, which sanction was never to be granted unless the trees were neither ornamental nor useful as protectors of springs. Neither rule did much good, apparently. In 1868, Mr.Breeks, who had recently been appointed as Commissioner of the district, said 'Day by day I feel more satisfied that, unless conservancy is taken in hand and organized on some efficient footing under the control of an experienced officer, the destruction of the surrounding sholas is but a question of time.'

From 1st April 1869 the Government sanctioned the transfer for the woods and plantations on the plateau to the Commissioner's care, the Jungle Conservancy Rules being introduced into them.

In 1875, the woods were retransferred to the Forest Department, under the care of which they have ever since remained. But the destruction of the woodlands round the stations which had come into private hands either by purchase from the Badagas or by sales under the Waste Land Rules went on as before; and in January 1878 a Commission was appointed to report what forests might be regularly reserved. Eventually Government decided in 1880 to reserve strictly the whole of the woods remaining on their Plateau, which by now except on the west, of small extent.

But no demarcation of these woods on the ground was provided for, their boundaries being merely marked on the maps; and when, in 1882, the Forest Act was introduced, the selection, mapping and demarcation of the reserves had for the most part to be done afresh.

The figures in the margin show the extents now finally protected. The percentage of the area of Gudalur taluk (an almost unbroken sea of Jungle) which is reserved is small because so much of the land there has been declared to be private janmam property).

Taluk	*Area of reserves in square miles*	*Percentage to total area of Taluk*
Coonoor	74	31
Ootacamund	300	68
Gudalur	30	11
Total	404	42

Nilgiris landscape at present, is dominated by the eucalyptus tree. Francis records the advent and spread of these exotic trees.

The Government's efforts to preserve the woodlands have been immensely furthered by the extensive planting of Australian trees for firewood which has been undertaken officially and by private agency. The Australian black wood (Acacia melanoxylon) wattle (A. dealbata) were first introduced about 1832. In 1853 the systematic planting of black wood and wattle was begun in the neighbourhood of Wellington, but it was not until 1856 that Captain (now General) Morgan imported a quantity of blue gum seed from Australia, set to work to sow some of it on a definite plan on the Tudor Hall estate, and distributed the rest among the settlers on the hills. Even by 1857 black wood and wattle were so scarce that plants of them were sold at the Government Gardens at four annas a piece, while blue gum plants fetched as much as twelve annas. These three trees have since then altered the whole appearance of the Nilgiri hill-stations, and acres of land which appear in the old sketches and photographs as open grass are now covered with their gloomy foliage.

The first Government plantation of Australian trees in the district was made in 1856 near Bleak House, Wellington. In 1858 Government sanctioned the planting of 10,000 trees in and about Ootacamund for ornamental purposes and with the idea of encouraging tree-growing by private persons. Except about the borders of the lake, few of the trees then put down survive, and these few have been indifferently cared for. Thereafter Government fuel plantations were formed at an increasing rate. By 1869, when the forests of the plateau were put under Jungle Conservancy as already described, they covered 191 acres, and by 1875, when the forest department took charge, they had grown to 919 acres. Private planting had also been found to be very profitable and had proceeded space, and the cry to-day is not that three is any want of firewood (for trees barely pay for the felling) but that the houses in the stations are too often buried in masses of tall Australian trees which shut out light, air and the view.

Mudumalai forest is now a game sanctuary. It also contains valuable teak. Francis/Gazetteer records;

The Mudumalai forest (46,600 acres) is the janmam property of the Nilambur Tirumalpad and was leased from him by Government for five years from 1857 and again for 99 years from October 1863. The forest contains much teak, vengai, ven-teak and several of the Terminalias, particularly T. tomentosa and T.Chebula, while in the valleys are black wood and the large thorny bamboo (Bambusa arundinacea) and on the drier uplands Anogeissus latifolia and the smaller or male kind of bamboo (Dendrocalamus strictus) in lesser quantities. On the northern border, next to Mysore, large areas are covered only with coarse elephant grass through which fierce fires sweep annually; but in places the rather uncommon Shorea Tabura grows gregariously and is useful for posts, smaller timber, and mine props. In the ravines, the teak does splendidly, but the forest has suffered in the past from frequent fires and from indiscriminate felling. It was originally leased to a timber merchant who removed as far as possible all accessible timber that had any value. It was then worked by Government and with the Benne forest contributed the greater part of the timber for the Wellington barracks. When it was first leased in 1863 Kurumbas were employed to search out, fell and square any teak trees of sufficient size which they could find and these were then dragged out by elephants and sent to Masinigaudi and Ootacamund for sale. Even in 1863, it was reported that at the close of the year's operations 'little or no teak fit for extraction would be left'; but felling went on none the less.

In 1885, a beginning of better conservation was made. Parts of the forest were divided off and trees were felled in them in a more systematic manner, all big timber also all stunted and useless trees being removed to give the young teak as much light and air as possible and the compartment being then closed to cattle to allow of natural reproduction. Camping places were also fixed at definite spots in the hope of reducing the number of fires which occurred every dry season from people halting promiscuously in the forest. The system then inaugurated has been more or less adhered to since, but, as a late conservator put it, 'we cannot expect to make a large revenue from the improvement fellings; the plums have most effectually been picked out of the can'.

This brief glimpse into the past, gives us a perspective which helps in understanding the changing face of the district in response to economic pressures during the last 150 years. Rapid destruction of forests took place in the 19th century. While systematic efforts at conservation have slowed the rate of destruction, the decline in forest area and quality of green cover, continued in the present century. The Hill Area Development Programme represents serious efforts made after independence, towards preservation of what is left of the Nilgiris ecology and restoration of at least some of the degraded areas.

References

1. Francis W (1908) Madras District Gazetteer of the Nilgiris district, Government of Madras reprinted 1994 by Asian Educational Services, New Delhi-16.
2. Marshall WE (1873), 'A phrenologist among the Todas', Longmans Green and Company, London reprinted 1995 by Asian Educational Services, New Delhi-16.

12

Darjeeling and the Nilgiris—A Comparison

A description of the Nilgiris district has been given in Chapter 3. A historical perspective about the district has been given in Chapter 11. It would be interesting to compare the Nilgiris with another hill district in India. Comparison with a comparable hill district, viz., Darjeeling, was made through field visits and discussions with Planning Officials, Tea Board Officials and tea planters in Darjeeling during September 1999.

Both Ooty and Darjeeling attract a large number of tourists, nature lovers and honey-mooners. Both are compact hill districts. Both are known for salubrious climate and tea gardens. Mountain railways add charm to both the hill stations.

Darjeeling is located in the extreme north of the State of West Bengal. Located at 27° North-Latitude, Darjeeling has temperate climate. It borders Sikkim and Nepal. Darjeeling (2200m) is in the foot-hills of the Himalayas. High Himalayan peaks including Mt.Everest, Lhotse, Makalu and

Kanchenjunga which are over 8,000m high are visible from Darjeeling. They beckon the visitor and lure the mountaineer to greater heights.

The Nilgiris district in Tamil Nadu, has borders with Kerala and Karnataka. Ooty (2300 m) is not much lower than the highest peak in the region (Doddabetta 2549 m). The visitor gets the feeling that he has climbed to the top of the hills. Ooty is at 11° 20' North-latitude, but enjoys sub-tropical climate because of the altitude.

Area of Darjeeling district is 2476 Sq.Km, very close to that of the Nilgiris (2,549 Sq.Km). Population of Darjeeling district is 6.94 lakhs (1991) which is similar to 7.10 lakhs of the Nilgiris. The Nilgiris district has a high percentage of S.C.(30%) while Darjeeling has a high percentage of S.T. (11%) population. Literacy of Nilgiris district (71.7%) is higher than that of Darjeeling (47%). Between the towns, Darjeeling's population of 71,470 is only slightly less than that of Ooty (81,763). Both are old hill stations and popular tourist spots.

Himalayas are regarded as relatively young mountains. Land-slides are common in Darjeeling. Road and rail links are frequently disturbed. The Deccan Plateau is said to be relatively stable. Earthquakes are unknown but land-slides still occur frequently in the Nilgiris, due to a variety of causes.

Introduction of tea in Darjeeling is attributed to one Dr.Campbell, who was the first superintendent of Darjeeling town. He is said to have planted a few tea seeds of the China stock in early 1841 near his bungalow. The first commercial plantation dates from 1856. Within 10 years, 4,000 hectares were under tea. Tea cultivation is labour intensive. Most of the workers in tea gardens are Gurkhas from Nepal attracted by the wages paid by the Planters. It is said that they were made to believe that 'in Darjeeling, money grows in tea bushes.'

According to Tea Board Statistics for 1993, Darjeeling had 19,324 Ha of tea gardens, as compared to 26,423 in the Nilgiris. Darjeeling produced only 13 million kg. of tea-leaves during that year while the Nilgiris produced 78.9 million kg. The average yield in Darjeeling was only 640 Kgs./Ha while it was 2,785 Kg./Ha in the Nilgiris. Productivity in the Nilgiris was more than 4 times that of Darjeeling.

Tea gardens are numerous in the Nilgiris. While Darjeeling had only 79 gardens in 1993, Nilgiris had 6,785. In Darjeeling 64 out of 79 gardens were of 100 hectares or more. In the Nilgiris, only 55 out of 6,785 were 100 hectares or more in extent. Such large gardens accounted for over 18,000 Ha out of 19,324 in Darjeeling. But in the Nilgiris, 14,750 Ha, out of 26,423 were included in such large estates. While over 93% of the tea area in Darjeeling was with such large gardens, the corresponding figure for the Nilgiris was about 55% only. In contrast, small growers with less than 8 Ha, numbered 6585 in the Nilgiris and accounted for 8254 Ha. Small growers accounted for over 97% of the number and over 37% of the area in Nilgiris. There was no garden of such small size in Darjeeling.

While tea cultivation in Darjeeling is dominated by the large gardens, the scene in the Nilgiris is dominated by small growers.

Tea cultivated near the equator, flushes throughout the year. Further from the equator, at latitudes beyond 16° the bushes remain completely dormant during the winter. Darjeeling is at 27° N-Latitude. Flushing season is from March to November. It experiences severe winter from December to February, when frosts are common. Ooty is 11° 20' latitude. Tea in Ooty flushes throughout the year with seasonal variations.

While tea grown in Darjeeling is of the China variety, that in the Nilgiris is of the Assam variety. There is a substantial area in the Nilgiris under clonal plantation.

Darjeeling tea is known for flavour, but has low productivity. While Nilgiris tea has a good flavour characteristic of high altitude tea, Nilgiris gardens also have the highest figures of productivity per Ha.

While tea area is static or slowly declining in Darjeeling, it is growing fast in the Nilgiris.

Much of the tea in the north-east is grown at lower altitudes and plains. But Darjeeling tea, known for its typical flavour is grown at high altitudes from 300 to 1900 meters. Rainfall varies between 2000 to 4500 mm in different valleys of Darjeeling district. The economy of the district is based primarily on the 'muscatel' flavour teas produced by tea estates situated on the mountain slopes. Darjeeling has more than 19,000 Ha under tea. More than half of the tea is of China (Camellia Sinensis) or China hybrid, the rest being largely of Cambod and Assam hybrid. A very small area is under clonal plantation. The produce of Darjeeling is often referred to as the 'champagne of teas'. It holds the pride of place in the world and is the image-bearer of tea exports from India.

Total annual production of tea in Darjeeling is of the order of 13 million Kg. The average yield of 640 Kg/Ha is very low in comparison with the average of 1650 Kg/Ha for the North-East and 2785 Kg/Ha for the Nilgiris. One of the reasons for low yield is the physical structure of the China hybrid type, which is grown in 50% of the tea area in Darjeeling. In this variety of tea, the shoots are very small. About 12,500 shoots of two leaves and a bud from these bushes, make one kilogram of tea. Broad leaf Assam tea of the same weight, has less than half this number of shoots.

Unlike tea gardens in the plains of North Eastern India, most of the tea gardens in Darjeeling are very old. Over 82% of the tea area in the district is over 50 years old. The yield of old areas is mostly very low, static or declining. Many estates have not taken up much of replanting or extension. Consequently the area under old and worn-out tea gardens is increasing to the detriment of productivity. Generally tea bushes over 50 years' old are past their productive life. The high percentage of such area (82%) in Darjeeling compares unfavourably with the similar figure (43%) for the national average. Darjeeling has a substantial area where tea bushes are over 100 years old, are quite unproductive and uneconomical.

Because of poor management, the vacancy of the bushes in existing gardens in Darjeeling is high. As against the all India average of 15%, the figure for Darjeeling is in excess of 20%. It has been estimated, that vacancies in Darjeeling are cumulatively of the order of 4,000 Ha.

Tea production in Darjeeling is affected by advanced age of the bushes, low productivity, poor management and high vacancies. Efforts are on to bring about increases in productivity in the district. In the meanwhile, the produce of Darjeeling, which is a mere 2% of the tea production in India, continues to spread its flavour all over the world. The quality of Darjeeling tea has remained unbeatable, incomparable and unique in flavour, ever-since it became famous. The productivity of Darjeeling Tea is only $^1/_3$ of that in the plains. While productivity should be increased, the quality and unique flavour of Darjeeling tea should be preserved.

Planning and Development of Darjeeling Hill district is under the charge of the Darjeeling Gorkha Hill Council. The area of jurisdiction of the Hill Council comprises of 2476 Sq. Km. in Kalimpong, Kurseong and Darjeeling sub-divisions and some villages of Siliguri sub-division. The area is slightly more than that of the area of the revenue district of Darjeeling. Among development departments, the activities of the Departments of Industries, Commerce, Power, Co-operatives, Forests and Highways remain with the State

Government. Other development departments are managed by the Hill Council.

Annual action plan of the Hill Council for 1997-98 had an outlay of Rs. 75.98 crores. Of this Rs. 59.64 crores was Special Central Assistance. Another Rs. 6.89 crores came from centrally sponsored schemes and only Rs. 9.55 crores from the State Plan. In contrast, outlay in the Nilgiris on HADP during 1997-98 was only Rs. 21.40 crores. While both districts are comparable in size (both are about 2,500 Sq.Km) and population (about 7 lakhs), the central assistance for the Nilgiris (Rs. 21.40 crores) is considerably less than that provided to Darjeeling (Rs. 59.64 crores).

A study of the annual action plan for Darjeeling reveals that emphasis is on sectors quite different from those on which the Nilgiris district is concentrating. About 33.8% of the outlay is on communications including road. 21.5% is on Tourism. 12.3% is on General Services. 5.7% is on Education. 4.6% is on Health. 24% of the outlay is distributed among 17 other sectors. One does not see the high emphasis on Forestry (only 2.8%), Horticulture (included in forests) and Soil conservation (0.7%) as seen in the plan for the Nilgiris district where over 50% of the outlay is on these three sectors.

Substitution of annual and seasonal crops by tea is an important scheme under HADP in the Nilgiris. But in Darjeeling, the plan of the Hill Council does not touch tea. This may be because there are no small tea farmers in Darjeeling, while their number is very large in the Nilgiris.

Comparison of the sectoral composition of the plans of the two districts leads us to the conclusion that the plan for Darjeeling aims at economic development, while that of the Nilgiris district aims at sustainable development of the district.

Salient statistical features and annual plans of the two districts are given in the tables below:-

COMPARISON OF SALIENT STATISTICS

	Darjeeling	*Nilgiris*
Area	2,476 Sq.Km.	2,549 Sq.Km.
Towns	4	4
Population	6,93,793	7,04,827
Rural	5,33,413 (76.9%)	3,53,746 (50.2%)
Urban	1,60,380 (23.1%)	3,51,081 (49.8%)
Darjeeling Town	71,470	Ooty Town : 81,763
Percentage of S.C. population	6.38%	30.3%
Percentage of S.T. population	10.99%	4%
Percentage of Literates	47.07%	71.7%
Forest Area	1,102 Sq.Km.(44.5%)	1,434 Sq.Km.(56.3%)
Area of Tea gardens	18,979 Ha	26,423 Ha
Area of holdings with less than 8.09 Ha	Nil	8,254 Ha (31.24%)
Area of holdings with more than 100 Ha	18,000 Ha (94.8%)	14,750 Ha (55.83%)
Number of gardens	79	6,785
Number of gardens of less than 8.09 Ha	Nil	6,585 (97%)
Number of gardens of extent over 100 Ha	64 (81%)	55 (0.8%)
Total Production	13 million Kg.	78.9 million Kg.
Average Production	640 Kg./Ha	2,785 Kg./Ha

Source: 1. The Statistics 1993-94. Tea Board, Calcutta, for Tea related statistics.
2. Annual Action plans of Nilgiris and Darjeeling districts for other data.

COMPARISON OF ANNUAL ACTION PLANS 1997-98

(Rs. in lakhs)

		Darjeeling		Nilgiris	
1.	Agriculture including soil conservation	89	1.17%	241 (Horti-culture) 428 (Soil conservation)	11.26% 20%
2.	Animal Resources Development	174	2.29%	45	2.10%
3.	Communication including Roads	2281	30.02%	297	13.88%
4.	Cottage & Small Industries	165	2.17%	17	0.79%
5.	District Improvement Fund	20	0.26%	—	—
6.	Education	592	7.79%	—	—
7.	Energy	10	0.13%	—	—
8.	Fisheries	144	1.89%	—	—
9.	Forest including Parks & Gardens	280	3.68%	337	15.75%
10.	General Services	893	11.75%	—	—
11.	Health	380	5.00%	40	1.87%
12.	Information and Culture	33	0.43%	—	—

Contd.

(Rs. in lakhs)

		Darjeeling		*Nilgiris*	
13.	Irrigation	254	3.34%	—	—
14.	Labour	25	0.33%	—	—
15.	Minor Irrigation	70	0.92%	100	4.67%
16.	Public Health Engineering	285	3.75%	100	4.67%
17.	Rural Development	200	2.63%	—	—
18.	SC/ST Welfare	30	0.39%	100	4.67%
19.	Sports & Youth Services	210	2.76%	80	3.74%
20.	Transport	10	0.13%	—	—
21.	Tourism	1353	17.80%	80	3.74%
22.	Urban Development	100	1.32%	—	—
23.	Others	—	—	275	12.85%
	Total	7598	100%	2140	100%

Source: Annual Action Plans of Darjeeling and Nilgiris districts.

References

1. Ghosh Hajra N. (1992), 'Strategies for improvement of Tea production in Darjeeling Hills', Indian Review, Life Sciences 12 : 195 - 210

2. Datta Ranen, (1996), 'Darjeeling Tea', District Tea Planters' Association, Darjeeling

3. Darjeeling Gorkha Hill Council (1997), 'Annual Action Plan 1997-98' unpublished

4. 'Tea Statistics 1993-94', Tea Board, Calcutta.

Bibliography

Books

- Anderson T and Leal D.R.,(1990), Free Market Environmentalism, Pacific Research Institute for Public Policy, San Francisco.
- Arkin H and Colton R, (1959), Statistical Method, Barnes and Noble, New York.
- Banskota M and Partap T (1992), Education Research and Sustainable Mountain Agriculture, International Centre for Integrated Mountain Development, Kathmandu.
- CSWRTI, (1972), Package of practices for soil and water conservation in the Deccan-Nilgiris region, Central Soil and Water Conservation Research and Training Institute, Ootacamund.
- CSWRTI, (1980), Rainfall frequency Atlas of the Nilgiris, Central Soil and Water Research and Training Institute, Ooty.
- CSWRTI (1982), 25 years research on soil and water conservation in southern high rainfall region, CSWRTI.
- Francis, W (1908), Madras District Gazetter of the Nilgiris District, Government of Madras reprinted 1994 by Asian Educational Services, Hauz Khas, New Delhi.

- Gadgil M and Guha R, (1993), This Fissured land – an ecological history of India, Oxford University Press, Delhi.
- Government of India (1980), Sixth Five Year Plan 1980-85, Planning Commission, New Delhi.
- Government of India (1982), The Nilgiris Landslide, Geological Survey of India, Calcutta.
- Government of India (1985), Seventh Five Year Plan, 1985-90, Planning Commission, New Delhi.
- Government of India (1992), Eighth Five Year Plan 1992-97.
- Government of India (1997), A report on the land-slide inventory in Nilgiris District, Geological Survey of India, Calcutta.
- Government of Tamil Nadu (1994), Department of Statistics, Statistical Handbook of Tamil Nadu 1994.
- Gujarati Damodar (1991), Basic Econometrics, McGraw Hill, New York.
- IFPRI (1995) A 2020 vision for Food Environment, International Food Policy Research Institute and the National Geographic Society, Washington, D.C.
- ICRA, (1996), The Indian Tea Industry, ICRA, Industry Water series #2, ICRA Investment Information Publication, New Delhi-2.
- Jodha N.S. Banskota M and Partap T Ed (1996), Sustainable Mountain Agriculture, Oxford and IBH Publication, New Delhi.
- Marshall WE (1873), A phrenologist among the Todas, Longman Green, London reprinted 1995 by Asian Educational Services, Haus Khas, New Delhi.

- Mood AM, Graybill F.A. and Boes D.C. (1974), Introduction to the theory of Statistics, Mc Graw Hill, Singapore.
- Mukherjee A and Agnihotri V.K. Ed (1995), Environment and Development (view from the East and West), Concept Publishing, New Delhi-59.
- Muthaiah S (1993), A Planting Century – the first hundred years of UPASI, Affiliated East West Press, Chennai-10.
- Statistical Hand book of Tamil Nadu, 2003, Department of Economics and Statistics, Government of Tamil Nadu
- Tea Board (1995), Tea Statistics 1993-94, Tea Board Calcutta
- WCED (1987), 'Our Common Future' Report of the World Commission on Environment and Development, Oxford University Press, New York.

Published Papers

- Chand Ramesh (1996), "Ecological and Economic impart of Horticultural Development in the Himalayas", *Economic and Political Weekly, June 29, 1996.*
- Datta Ranen, (1996), 'Darjeeling Tea', District Tea Planters' Association, Darjeeling.
- Ghosh Hajra N (1992), "Strategies for improvement of tea production in Darjeeling Hills", *Indian Review, Life Sciences 12.*
- Gohlert Ernest, (1993), *Foundation of Sustainable Development,* Proceedings of the International Conference on Sustainable Village Based

Development, Colorado State University, Fort Collins, USA.

- Pranesh M.B. (1993), *Sustainable Village Based Development – Central Government Policy – The Indian Picture*, Proceeding of the International Conference on Sustainable Village Based Development, Colorado State University, Fort Collins, USA, pp. 505-519.
- Rao U.R. (1995), "Statistical Dynamics of Sustainable Development", *Man and Development*, Vol. XVII No.2, June 95, Centre for Research in Rural and Industrial Development.
- Sachs Ignacy,(1995), "Searching for new development Strategies – Challenges of the Social Summit", *Economic and Political Weekly*, July 8, 1995, pp. 1682-91.

Reports and Others

- Anna University, *Macro-evaluation of the impact of HADP*, Institute of Remote Sensing, Chennai – 25.
- Annual Plan Proposals of HADP, Planning Development & Special Initiatives Department, Government of Tamil Nadu, unpublished
- CSWCRTI (1982), *Soil and Water Conservation in Southern Hill regions of India*, Proceedings of working group – Central Soil and Water Conservation Research and Training Institute, Ootacamund.
- Darjeeling Gorkha Hill Council (1997), 'Annual Action Plan 1997-98', unpublished
- Directorate of Evaluation and Applied Research (DEAR) (1990), *Report on a quick evaluation of check*

dams constructed by PWD under minor irrigation component of HADP in Nilgiris District, Government of Tamil Nadu.

- DEAR (1991), *Evaluation report on Re-clothing the slopes in the degraded forest under HADP in Nilgiris District*, Government of Tamil Nadu.
- DEAR (1992), *Evaluation study on sanctuary for rosewood and its associates under HADP in the Nilgiris District*, Government of Tamil Nadu.
- DEAR (1993), *Evaluation report on eco-protection for degraded Sholas and endangered species by chain link fencing in Nilgiris district under HADP*, Government of Tamil Nadu.
- DEAR (1995), *Evaluation report on schemes for providing assistance to tea with special reference to modernization of tea factories*, Govt. of Tamil Nadu.
- DEAR (1995) (2), *Evaluation report on rural water supply under HADP*, Government of Tamil Nadu.
- DEAR (1996), *Draft evaluation report on artificial insemination and morbidity pattern under animal husbandry sector – HADP*, Govt. of Tamil Nadu.
- Government of India (1997), *Integrated Mission for Sustainable Development of the Nilgiris District*, Department of Space, Bangalore.
- Government of Tamil Nadu (1992), *HADP Annual Plan proposals 1992-97*, Planning and Development Department, Chennai-9.
- Government of Tamil Nadu (1994), (2), *HADP Annual Plan proposals 1994-95*, Planning and Development Department, Chennai-9.

- Government of Tamil Nadu (1995), *HADP Annual Plan proposals 1995-96*, Planning and Development Department, Chennai-9.
- Government of Tamil Nadu (1996), *HADP Annual Plan proposals 1996-97*, Planning and Development Department, Chennai-9.
- Government of Tamil Nadu (1997), *Kundah and Lower Bhavani River Valley Project – appraisal cum evaluation report* – Chief Engineer, Agricultural Engineering Department, Anna Salai, Chennai-35.
- HADP (1997), *HADP Nilgiris/An Approach Paper*, HADP Cell, Ootacamund.
- HADP (1997) (2), *A note on Geo-technical activities*, Geotechnical Cell, HADP, Coonoor.
- INCOSERVE (1997), *Short notes on the performance of Industrial tea Co-operative societies in the Nilgiris district*, INCOSERVE, Coonoor.
- J Thomas, 2001, J.Thomas & Company Private Limited, "Tea Market Annual Report and Statistics 2001"
- Mishra Committee Report, 2000, Government of Tamil Nadu, unpublished
- NABARD (1998), *Potential linked credit plan – Nilgiris district*, National Bank for agriculture and Rural Development, Regional office, Chennai-6.
- Price Waterhouse (1997), *HADP Evaluation Final Report*, 610 Anna Salai, Chennai-6.
- Ramu S and Ramamoorthy, G (1997), *Promotion of tea cultivation for crop diversification in Nilgiris*, Paper presented at Workshop organised by HADP, Ootacamund.

- Roy Choudhury (1997), *A note on Tea Board financial assistance schemes for the development of small tea growers' sector in South India*, Tea Board, Regional Office, Coonoor.
- Saptharishi Committee, 2003, Report of the Inter-Ministerial Committee constituted by the Ministry of Labour to look into the various issues relating to the Plantation Sector in India, Government of India, unpublished
- Save Nilgiris Campaign (1991), *Intensive environment education – a pilot project*, Save Nilgiris Campaign, Ootacamund.
- Shri AMM Murugappa Chettiar Research Centre (1990), *Project Kurinji, Nilgiris Integrated renewable energy perspective*, Photosynthesis and Energy division, Tharamani, Chennai-113.
- TANTEA (1998), *A note on the activities of TANTEA*, The Tamil Nadu Tea Plantations Corporation Limited, Coonoor.
- Tata Consultancy Services (1994), *Perspective Plan for the Western Ghats Development Programme*, TCS, Bishop Wallers Avenue (East), Chennai-4.
- Tea Board, 2003, "Situation prevailing in the tea industry in South India" an article by Shri Vikram Kapur, I.A.S, Executive Director, Tea Board, unpublished.
- TNAU (1996), *An evaluation study on the impact of Small tea-growers' development schemes of Tea Board in South India*, Department of Agricultural Economics, Tamil Nadu Agricultural University, Coimbatore.
- UPASI (1995), *The Planters' Voice*, September 1995, The United Planters' Association of South India, Coonoor-101.

- UPASI (1997), *Importance of Plantation Crops in South India*, The United Planters' Association of South India, Coonoor-101.
- UPASI (1997), (2), *An overview of Tea Industry and Trade*, UPASI.
- UPASI, 2003, The United Planters' Association of Southern India, "Emerging Trends in the Plantation Sector" September 2003.

Index

CBP 24/10/05